Physics Students' book and Teachers' guide **Unit 10**

Waves, particles, and atoms

0 582 82714 0
Nuffield Advanced Science

Nuffield Advanced Physics team

Joint organizers

Dr P. J. Black, Reader in Crystal Physics, University of Birmingham

Jon Ogborn, Worcester College of Education; formerly of Roan School, London SE3

Team members

W. Bolton, formerly of High Wycombe College of Technology and Art

R. W. Fairbrother, Centre for Science Education, Chelsea College; formerly of Hinckley Grammar School

G. E. Foxcroft, Rugby School

Martin Harrap, formerly of Whitgift School, Croydon

Dr John Harris, Centre for Science Education, Chelsea College; formerly of Harvard Project Physics

Dr A. L. Mansell, Centre for Science Education, Chelsea College; formerly of Hatfield College of Technology

A. W. Trotter, North London Science Centre; formerly of Elliott School, Putney

Evaluation

P. R. Lawton, Garnett College, London

Acknowledgements

The Organizers wish to thank the following people, who gave their time to reading a draft of this book, met to discuss it, and gave us much invaluable advice:

Professor Sir Nevill Mott, Professor R. W. Chambers, Professor P. T. Matthews, Professor M. M. Woolfson, Dr V. I. Little, Dr H. Post

We also wish to thank the Director and staff of the Atlas Computer Laboratory, Chilton, and particularly Dr F. R. A. Hopgood, for their help in bringing to fruition the computer-made film used in Part Three.

Every book of this kind relies heavily on the work of other people. We have learned much from the work of PSSC; from *The Feynman lectures on physics*; from C. W. Sherwin's *Basic concepts of physics*; from the article by Professor Sir Nevill Mott, 'On teaching quantum phenomena'; and from an early draft of *Physics – a new introductory course*, written for the M.I.T. introductory physics course by Professor A. P. French.

Physics Students' book and Teachers' guide Unit 10

Waves, particles, and atoms

Nuffield Advanced Science
Published for the Nuffield Foundation by Longman Group Limited

LONGMAN GROUP LIMITED
Longman House
Burnt Mill, Harlow, Essex. U. K.

First published 1971
Fourth impression 1981
ISBN 0 582 82714 0

Designed by Ivan and Robin Dodd
Illustrations designed and produced
by Penguin Education

Printed in Hong Kong
by Wing Tai Cheung Printing Co Ltd.

Contents

Nuffield Advanced Physics team and special advisers *ii*

Foreword *vii*

About this book *1*

Introduction: the quantum revolution *3*

Part One
Photons *5*

Part Two
Electrons *41*

Part Three
Waves in boxes *61*
Stage one   Order of magnitude arguments about hydrogen and about nuclei *65*
Stage two   Electron standing waves in a $1/r$ shaped 'box' *76*
Stage three   Schrödinger's equation for electron waves in atoms *95*

Part Four
The scope of wave mechanics *113*

Postscript
A personal note on the origin and future of quantum mechanics
by Professor Sir Nevill Mott *133*

Appendix
The Compton effect: a photo-electric game of billiards *137*

More questions *145*

Answers *149*
Part One *150*
Part Two *152*
Part Three *153*
Answers to 'More questions' *156*

Lists of films, film loops, books, and apparatus
Films and film loops *160*
Books *161*
Apparatus *162*

Index *164*

Foreword

It is almost a decade since the Trustees of the Nuffield Foundation decided to sponsor curriculum development programmes in science. Over the past few years a succession of materials and aids appropriate to teaching and learning over a wide variety of age and ability ranges has been published. We hope that they may have made a small contribution to the renewal of the science curriculum which is currently so evident in the schools.

The strength of the development has unquestionably lain in the most valuable part that has been played in the work by practising teachers and the guidance and help that have been received from the consultative committees to each Project.

The stage has now been reached for the publication of materials suitable for Advanced courses in the sciences. In many ways the task has been a more difficult one to accomplish. The sixth form has received more than its fair share of study in recent years and there is now an increasing acceptance that an attempt should be made to preserve breadth in studies in the 16–19 year age range. This is no easy task in a system which by virtue of its pattern of tertiary education requires standards for the sixth form which in many other countries might well be found in first year university courses.

Advanced courses are therefore at once both a difficult and an interesting venture. They have been designed to be of value to teacher and student, be they in sixth forms or other forms of education in a similar age range. Furthermore, it is expected that teachers in universities, polytechnics, and colleges of education may find some of the ideas of value in their own work.

If this Advanced Physics course meets with the success and appreciation I believe it deserves, it will be in no small measure due to a very large number of people, in the team so ably led by Jon Ogborn and Dr Paul Black, in the consultative committee, and in the schools in which trials have been held. The programme could not have been brought to a successful conclusion without their help and that of the examination boards, local authorities, the universities, and the professional associations of science teachers.

Finally, the Project materials could not have reached successful publication without the expert assistance that has been received from William Anderson and his editorial staff in the Nuffield Science Publications Unit and from the editorial and production teams of Penguin Education.

K. W. Keohane
Co-ordinator of the Nuffield Foundation Science Teaching Project

About this book

This book is written for both students and teachers. There are experiments suggested in it, but the main work is theoretical. We have tried to write it in such a way that teacher and student may think through the theory together. For that purpose, many of the arguments are presented in the form of chains of questions. Each question is, however, answered at the back of the book, so that no one need be 'lost'. This is not a book for those who expect to sit back and watch someone else doing the work, and it contains much practical workaday physics, but it is physics done with the head, rather than with the hands.

There are a number of passages, enclosed in ruled boxes like the sample that follows, which are comments or information meant mainly for teachers.

Using this book in the classroom

This book contains work intended to interest the best students, which goes further than most students need, or will wish to go. Parts One and Two, and Part Three up to the end of stage one, page 75, contain the main material of the book. It is not essential for anyone to do more than this, and compulsory examination questions would be restricted to this material. We think that all students should see just a little of 'Part Four, which tries to indicate the width and scope of the results, studied earlier in rather close detail, so that they may see quantum physics in a broader perspective.

Stages two and three of Part Three are provided for students who are not satisfied with the crude arguments of Part Three, stage one. They should not be forced on anyone, but we hope that a proportion of students will enjoy exercising their skill and ability to the full by following through one or both of these extra sections. Stage two is within the capacity of most students, provided there is time for it. Stage three is tougher, but has the merit of drawing together and using a number of the pieces of mathematics developed earlier in the course.

Teachers will, of course, use this book as they think best. Some groups of questions may be used for homework, or class discussion. Teachers may wish to expound certain parts, leaving students to read the same material later, or they may prefer students to read in advance of the teaching. Others may wish to run a seminar system, with the class work being mainly discussion of work read beforehand.

The approach to quantum physics

Part One discusses the problem of wave-particle duality for photons, and also links the study of photons with earlier work on energy levels, showing how energy level schemes can be derived from spectra. Part Two shows that electrons share with photons the same puzzling dual behaviour, by way of experiments on electron diffraction.

Part Three puts these ideas to use in building a theory of the hydrogen atom. The first, crudest attempt in this direction simply treats an atom as a hard-edged box into which standing waves have to be fitted somehow or other. It is followed by a slightly better version, which takes note of the $1/r$ variation of potential, and shows how the Balmer $1/n^2$ rule arises as a consequence. Finally, for the few, there is a further discussion based on a simple numerical solution of a one-dimensional Schrödinger equation.

Part Four is intended, by way of examples including the helium ion, the hydrogen ion molecule, the patterns of ionization energy in the Periodic Table, oscillating molecules, and alpha decay, to indicate in a general fashion the scope and power of quantum theory.

Introduction: the quantum revolution

The years 1900 to 1930 saw a revolution overtake physics, comparable to the revolution brought about by Newton two centuries earlier. This Unit is about that revolution. Before Newton, the Sun and the planets were a puzzle. They obeyed known laws — the laws of Kepler — but no one knew why. After Newton, the solar system could be explained, and all that was needed to explain it were the laws of motion and the law of gravitation. Everything else followed as a consequence. The quantum revolution was comparable. Before 1900, many scientists believed that atoms existed, though some, notably Ostwald and Mach, were not sure one could believe any such thing.

But no one knew why the atoms of any one element had the properties they did have. After the period 1926 to 1930, there was a theory of these things, and papers came thick and fast, showing how to explain the spectra of elements, chemical bonds, electrical conductivity, magnetism, the nature of solids, and many other matters. Chemistry suddenly seemed explicable, though it has in the event turned out rather hard to get good quantitative predictions for many reactions.

These discoveries were made by finding that all was not well with the deepest laws of the physics of 1900, especially Newton's Laws and the wave theory of light. Richard Feynman, as a working physicist, has this to say about what happened:

> 'Then it was also found that the rules for the motions of particles were incorrect. The mechanical rules of "inertia" and "forces" are *wrong* — Newton's laws are wrong — in the world of atoms. Instead it was discovered that things on a small scale behave *nothing like* things on a large scale. That is what makes physics difficult — and very interesting. It is hard because the way things behave on a small scale is so "unnatural"; we have no direct experience with it. Here things behave like nothing we know of, so that it is impossible to describe this behaviour in any other than [mathematical] ways. It is difficult, and takes a lot of imagination.'
> *R. P. Feynman*

Other reading

This quotation comes from *The Feynman lectures on physics*, Volume 1. You will find that Chapters 1 to 3 give a valuable overall view of the nature and achievements of physics, and that they are well worth the effort of reading.

On several occasions in this book we shall suggest that you read some parts of other books. There are several reasons why this might be a good thing. No one book is likely to be perfect. Another book will often give a new and helpful perspective, quite apart from the fact that any one book may be wrong. The quantum idea is so strange and so important that many of the best physicists, including some of those who were responsible for the original ideas, have tried to write about it. Their efforts are likely to be much better than ours, and there can be especial value in direct contact with the people who first worked on the problems. In later years, whether you learn more physics or more of another subject, books will be your main source of new knowledge, and it is likely that some practice now will make it easier to learn by reading later on. (In the list on page 161, you will find details of reading recommended in the text.)

We do not suggest that you ought all to read all of the books mentioned. In a class of several students, each might read one or two on any one topic, and tell the others about what they say. The task of having to report on a book may itself help you to read more critically.

The work of this Unit

This Unit will try to show where the strange new quantum ideas came from. They will be used in a series of problems, showing how it is possible to explain the spectrum and energy levels of an atom, and to indicate how more complicated matters — like chemical bonds or random radioactive decay — may be understood. To reach that point, we shall have to discuss how it is that electrons behave like waves as well as like particles. But we start with something familiar, yet something that reveals all the peculiarity of the quantum world. We begin with light.

Part One

Photons

'*Query 8* Do not all fix'd Bodies, when heated beyond a certain degree, emit Light and shine; and is not this Emission perform'd by the vibrating motions of their parts?'

'*Query 29* Are not the Rays of Light very small Bodies emitted from shining substances?'

Isaac Newton (1730) Opticks.

'Suppose a number of equal waves of water to move upon the surface of a stagnant lake . . . and to enter a narrow channel leading out of the lake. Suppose then . . . another equal series of waves . . . arrive at the same channel . . .; if the elevations of one series . . . correspond to the depressions of the other, they must exactly fill up those depressions, and the surface of the water must remain smooth.

'Now I maintain that similar effects take place whenever two portions of light are thus mixed; and this I call the general law of the interference of light.'

Thomas Young (1804) 'Reply to the animadversions of the Edinburgh Reviewers on some papers published in the Philosophical Transactions (1804).'

. . . the energy in the light propagated by rays from a point is not smeared out continuously over larger and larger volumes, but rather consists of a finite number of energy quanta localized at space points, which move without breaking up and which can be absorbed or emitted only as wholes.

Albert Einstein (1905); translated from Annalen der Physik *17, 132.*

What is light?

The words of Newton, Young, and Einstein quoted on the previous page reveal a difference of opinion as to which of two models of light to adopt: the wave model or the particle model.

Earlier work in this course should have raised the same question. In Unit 8, *Electromagnetic waves,* the behaviour of light at narrow slits and the action of a diffraction grating were both explained by supposing light to be a wave. It was even possible to say something about what sort of wave light might be; one member of the family of electromagnetic waves.

Other evidence, however, has pointed in a different direction. When light shines on some metals, it ejects electrons from them, and the energy delivered seems to come in lumps or 'quanta', just as if there were something particle-like about the beam of light, properly described. You may have seen such evidence from the photo-electric effect, when you were working on Unit 5, *Atomic structure.*

In this Part, we shall see how, strangely enough, both models are needed. To begin with, we review some of the evidence.

Review of evidence 1
Long wavelength radiation does not do things that short wavelength radiation can do

Think about taking a photograph of a radio aerial. The aerials at Brookmans Park, near London, radiate 140 kilowatts of energy at a wavelength of 330 metres. They also reflect a little visible light energy. Only the latter affects the photographic emulsion, even though the visible light can have much less total energy. Similarly, if you photograph a car, even though the end containing the engine may be quite hot and will emit a good deal of infra-red radiant energy, the photograph does not usually show the bonnet 'brighter' than the rest of the car.

If it is a dull day, with little light energy available, one simply makes a longer exposure, and the photograph comes out. But however long the exposure, the infra-red and radio waves *never* affect the film. A similar experiment can be performed in the laboratory.

See Unit 4, *Waves and oscillations*, experiment 4.4, for details.

Figure 1 shows an experiment you may have seen. A diffraction grating or a prism splits up the light from a filament lamp into a spectrum of colours, which falls on a piece of photographic paper.

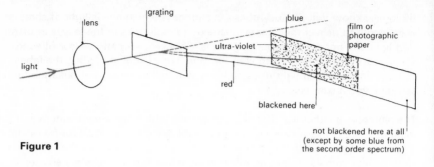

Figure 1

Q1   Which model of light explains the action of the grating better? Why?

This book contains many such questions. See the chapter 'Answers' (page 149).

Where there is yellow, green, or blue light on the paper, it blackens after development. It also blackens beyond the blue, being affected by yet shorter wavelength radiation, called ultra-violet radiation. But it does not blacken either in the red part, or in the warm, infra-red part of the spectrum. Yet there is plenty of energy in this long wavelength part of the spectrum, and even if there were not, a longer exposure is found to make no difference. Somehow, these rays are unable to affect the film. The film contains grains of silver halide each of which needs to have a certain energy delivered to it to produce a developable grain of silver.

Q2   Suppose the spectrum in the experiment above is made very faint. Do you think that any radiation which previously affected the paper will not do so now? How would you make a test?

Q3   Suppose radio waves did affect photographic film. What might be needed as well as a black paper wrapping to keep it unexposed? Is black paper good enough if the film is near a source of gamma rays?

There are other examples. Energy is needed to ionize atoms, as was shown by electron bombardment experiments in Unit 2, Part Five, when considering the evidence for the existence of energy levels. Experiments with X-rays or gamma rays show that they can ionize air, whilst ordinary visible light, however bright, is incapable of delivering the necessary energy to an individual 'air' molecule.

Biologists know that photosynthesis is a process which needs light of short enough wavelength to deliver the necessary energy to molecules in the leaves of plants. Red light will not do, however bright it is. Shopkeepers hang yellow filtering screens over their windows to stop the blue part of sunlight fading the fabrics on display. Yellow or red light does no harm. Nor will every kind of radiation from the sun give you a sun tan.

The situation is rather like that of a bus service which has a minimum fare. If the minimum fare is five pence, you cannot travel any distance at all for four pence, while you might be able to go several miles for five. Light is like that: red light (four pence) sometimes has no effect at all, while light of a slightly shorter wavelength will promptly produce results, like the five penny piece. Or it is like a slot machine that produces a cup of tea when a coin is inserted. A coin of half the value does not produce half a cupful; it produces nothing at all.

Review of evidence 2
The photo-electric effect

When light shines on some metals, electrons are ejected. The energy with which they come out can be measured, which is useful because we can relate this energy to the energy and frequency of the incoming light. The examples above were qualitative: this one can be made quantitative.

Q4 What is the advantage, in scientific inquiry, of a quantitative experiment which allows one to make measurements over one which can only be described in general terms?

Demonstration
10.1 Simple photo-electric cell

Demonstrations 10.1, 10.2, and 10.4 are identical with demonstrations from Unit 5 (5.16, 5.17, and 5.18). They may, or may not, all need to be done again.

1006	electrometer, with 10^{11} Ω input resistor, or 10^{-11} A range
1003/1	milliammeter (1 mA) for electrometer
1033	cell holder with four U2 cells
189	ultra-violet lamp
1056	magnesium ribbon 100 mm long
1055	glass plate
1055	wire gauze, 70 mm × 60 mm, for example, 20 mesh copper
503–6	retort stand base, rod, boss, and clamp
52 K	crocodile clip
1053	razor blade

Figure 2 shows a suitable arrangement. Scrape the magnesium ribbon with the razor blade to expose clean metal, turn over about 20 mm at one end, and push this end into the electrometer input socket.

Make a gauze cylinder 60 mm tall by wrapping the gauze round a former 15 to 20 mm in diameter. Turn out the last few millimetres, as shown in figure 2, to give a means of clamping the cylinder over the ribbon, and of making connection to the cylinder.

Using a 10^{11} Ω input resistor to the electrometer (current up to 10^{-11} A), there should be at least half scale deflection when the ultra-violet lamp is some 10 to 20 cm from the ribbon.

A glass plate absorbs the ultra-violet, and the current falls to zero. A copper or iron rod in place of the magnesium gives no photo-electric effect. Replacing the copper gauze with iron gauze makes no difference.

Some types of electrometer may be provided with a zinc plate and a gauze collector, with which the effect can be obtained using visible light.

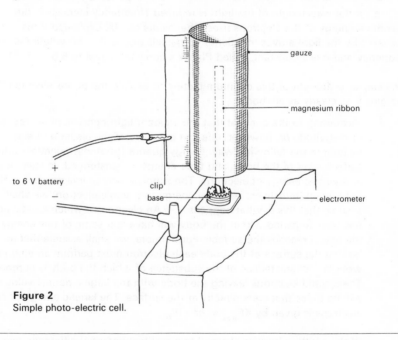

Figure 2
Simple photo-electric cell.

Experiments like this suggest that light of short enough wavelength can eject electrons from a metal, but that light of longer wavelength will not. It is not easy to find clear evidence which definitely settles upon one view of what is happening; indeed the photo-electric effect proved to be one of the more obstinate of the problems that experimentalists have tackled, right from the time of its discovery by Hertz. Hertz found that, when he was experimenting with his radio spark transmitter (you may have seen a similar one in Unit 8), the sparks came more readily when another spark gap was operating nearby. The effect was traced to the ultra-violet light from the second spark knocking electrons out of the metal making the gap for the first, and so starting off a conducting path in the gap.

It was a long while before the combined results of many experiments began to tell a clear story. The story they tell is as follows.

   a   Light of a certain colour is found to produce electrons with a certain definite maximum energy. Even though brighter light delivers energy at a faster rate, brighter light of that colour does *not* produce electrons with a greater energy; it produces *more* electrons with the *same* energy.

   b   Light of wavelength larger than a certain value (differing according to the metal used) produces *no* electrons, however bright it is.

   Q5   How does point **b** above compare with the spectrum photograph experiment, figure 1 ?

   c   If the wavelength of the light is reduced (frequency increased) the maximum energy of the electrons rises. The results can be explained if the energy E delivered by the light arrives in 'quanta' or parcels of size $E = hf$, where f is the frequency and h is a constant, called Planck's constant, equal to 6.6×10^{-34} J s.

Einstein, who thought of this quantum picture to explain the photo-electric effect, explains it as clearly as anybody:

> 'According to the concept that the incident light consists of energy quanta of magnitude hf, however, one can conceive of the ejection of electrons by light in the following way. Energy quanta (photons) penetrate into the surface layer of the body, and their energy is transformed, at least in part, into kinetic energy of electrons. The simplest way to imagine this is that a light quantum delivers its entire energy to a single electron; we shall assume that this is what happens. . . . An electron to which kinetic energy has been imparted within the body will have lost some of this energy by the time it reaches the surface. Furthermore, we shall assume that in leaving the surface of the body each electron must perform an amount of work W_0, characteristic of the substance of which the body is composed. The ejected electrons leaving the body with the largest normal velocity will be those that were directly at the surface. The kinetic energy of such electrons is given by $KE_{max} = hf - W_0$.
>
> 'If the emitting body is charged to a positive potential difference relative to a neighbouring conductor, and if V represents the potential difference which just stops the photo-electric current . . . [then]
> $$eV = hf - W_0$$
> where e denotes the electronic charge.

'If the deduced formula is correct, a graph of V versus the frequency of the incident light must be a straight line with a slope that is independent of the nature of the emitting substance. . . .

*(From Einstein, A., 1905, Annalen der Physik, **17**, 132, as reproduced in translation, in Arons (A.B. (1965))* Development of concepts of physics, Addison-Wesley. *(Einstein's symbols have been modified.*))

Q6 Having read Einstein's summary of the explanation of the photo-electric effect, by means of a quantum model, use it to calculate the minimum frequency of light needed to ionize a helium atom, whose ionization energy is about 24 electronvolts.

$$1 \text{ electronvolt} = 1.6 \times 10^{-19} \text{ J}$$
$$h = 6.6 \times 10^{-34} \text{ J s.}$$

When Einstein made this suggestion, the quantitative experimental evidence was by no means clear. When there was a definite quantitative prediction to test, however, experiments were done, and despite many difficulties, showed that the results fitted Einstein's ideas. Some of the best experiments were done by Millikan, and it is possible to repeat some of Millikan's experiments in the school laboratory, though absolutely clear-cut results must not be expected.

Reading

See Millikan, *The electron*, chapter X, for Millikan's description of his photo-electric measurements. These were the first reliable test of the linear relationship between maximum energy and frequency suggested by Einstein. His results are given on page 228 of the book.

Demonstration and long experiment
10.2 Colour of light and energy of photo-electrons

To test Einstein's ideas quantitatively, one must shine light on a clean metal surface for, if the surface is dirty, or if it is oxidized, the light has to try to remove electrons from a whole variety of different kinds of molecules on the surface, and the ejection of electrons from the metal is not what is being tested at all. In practice, this means having the metal in a vacuum and, ideally, cutting a clean surface just before the test. For a school experiment, it is good enough to use a photo-electric cell from which nearly all the air has been removed. The emitting surface will be some metal such as potassium, while the electrons will be collected on a metal, such as platinum, that does not emit electrons when light shines on it. You may well be able to detect effects in any experiments you see which would be explicable if the collector *were* emitting electrons. One reason for this is that the potassium tends to get deposited on the platinum collector to some extent. Such effects may tend to mask those you are hoping to see.

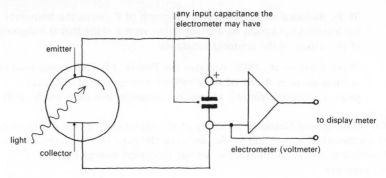

Figure 3
Circuit for a test of the photo-electric effect.

Test of Einstein's predictions

To test Einstein's ideas, it is necessary to measure the maximum energy with which electrons are emitted. One way to do this is to connect the photo-electric cell to an electrometer, which behaves as a voltmeter that draws next to no current, as shown in figure 3. As electrons are gathered by the collector, a potential difference builds up across the capacitance of the electrometer, and also across the photocell. The collector becomes negative, since electrons with negative charge are arriving there, and thus, as the potential difference builds up, it becomes harder and harder for more electrons to reach the collector. If the electrons, charge e, have a certain maximum kinetic energy, no more electrons will reach the collector when the potential difference V is given by

$$\text{maximum kinetic energy} = eV.$$

Thus, a big potential difference, V, recorded by the electrometer, indicates a large maximum energy of the electrons, and V is in direct proportion to the maximum kinetic energy as long as the electrometer records V without reducing it by drawing any current. The electrometer gives trouble when the light is dim, for the current is then small, and the electrometer always does draw some current, however little.

A good test is to sweep the various colours of the spectrum across the photocell. With red light, the potential difference is small, but it rises as the light shining on the cell is made bluer.

If one colour is chosen, and the light is made dimmer by cutting off some of it with a stop, the potential difference shows little if any change until the light is so feeble that the electrometer current begins to matter a good deal. Both results are what was predicted.

The Planck constant h

It would be nice to be able to try different metals in the photocell, and to test Einstein's predictions more thoroughly, but that would be a very ambitious undertaking. At least, the value of the Planck constant h can be estimated, from the potential differences V_1 and V_2 across the photocell when no electrons reach the collector, in light of frequencies f_1 and f_2. Whatever the energy W needed by an electron to escape from the metal,

$$hf_1 = eV_1 + W$$
and $$hf_2 = eV_2 + W.$$

From these equations:

$$h = \frac{e(V_2 - V_1)}{(f_2 - f_1)}.$$

The frequencies of the two colours of light have to be calculated from measurements, or estimates, of their wavelengths. Earlier in the course, you may well have measured h, whose value is 6.6×10^{-34} J s, in this way. In this Unit we shall see how important a constant it is: it will turn up in more than this one place. Like the charge on an electron, it is a fundamental constant. No one knows why it is has the value it does have, and physicists are not even able to see whether this would be a sensible question to ask, much as some would like to ask it. Maybe one day h will be linked up with other things in a way that helps to make sense of its value, but for the time being it is just one of those things that are as they are.

Demonstration and long experiment
10.2 Colour of light and energy of photo-electrons
(see experiment 5.17)

1068	parallel beam projector
59	l.t. variable voltage supply
69	high dispersion prism
1074	photo-electric cell
1006	electrometer
1003/1	milliammeter (1 mA) for electrometer
1033	cell holder with one U2 cell
1053	card with slit
1067 E	set of stops
1000	leads

Figure 4 shows an arrangement for projecting a spectrum of white light on the photocell. A slit in a card held over the photocell allows only a narrow range of wavelengths to enter the cell. Figure 3 shows a suitable circuit.

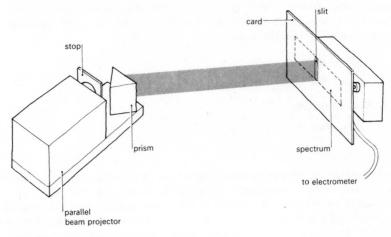

Figure 4
Projection of a spectrum on a photocell.

The slit should be about 2 mm wide, and should be centred on the aperture of the photocell. The parallel beam projector may be overrun by up to 30 per cent to obtain a bright spectrum. The spectrum should be formed at minimum deviation. Room lighting should be dim, and the photocell shielded from stray light.

The photocell may contain a battery and a potentiometer for reducing the cell current to zero by applying an external p.d. to it. In the method suggested here, these are not used; the cell develops its own p.d. across itself and the electrometer.

Before connecting the electrometer to the photocell, connect a 1.5 V dry cell across its input, and alter the sensitivity (gain) until the display meter reads full scale for this p.d. When connecting the electrometer to the photocell, join the positive going input to the potassium emitter, and remove any input resistor so that the electrometer functions as a voltmeter of the highest possible input resistance.

Variation with colour Start with the dark region of the spectrum beyond the red over the slit, and with the electrometer short-circuited. Then switch the electrometer to read the p.d. across its input terminals, when no appreciable reading should appear. Sweep the spectrum *slowly* across the slit, allowing time for the p.d. to rise at each step. The reading rises through the blue and into the ultra-violet. Beyond the ultra-violet it stays steady, even if the light is cut off, because there is no way for the electrometer input capacitance to discharge. If the electrometer is momentarily short-circuited, the reading falls to zero and stays there, if no radiation is entering the cell.

Warning A seemingly paradoxical result can be obtained by sweeping the spectrum back from blue to red, when the high reading falls steadily, though one would expect it not to, since low energy electrons produced by red light ought not to be able to reach the collector. The reason is that some potassium gets onto the collector, and it emits some electrons which flow the 'wrong' way. It is probably best to avoid the point by not sweeping the spectrum across the slit from blue to red.

To estimate the Planck constant h, note the electrometer indications V_1 and V_2 first when red light and then when violet light fall on the cell. Estimates of the wavelengths give an acceptable value of h, using $h = e(V_2 - V_1)/(f_2 - f_1)$.

Variation with brightness Shine the blue part of the spectrum on the slit. Reduce the intensity by placing stops over the lens of the projector, with the stops exactly over the centre of the lens (since an off centre stop produces a spectrum in a different place and alters the colour of the light falling on the slit). The p.d. should change by less than 10 per cent, though the intensity has changed by a much larger factor. If the intensity is reduced very much, the p.d. will fall much more, as the electrometer resistance becomes comparable to that of the photocell. The point needs to be admitted openly.

Energies of photons

The parcels or quanta of radiant energy, of size $E = hf$, can be calculated for different frequencies, given that $h = 6.6 \times 10^{-34}$ J s. This has been done in table 1. See Rogers, *Physics for the inquiring mind*, page 723, for a splendid drawing showing how big the quanta of various radiations are.

	Radio 2	3 cm microwaves	Visible light	Gamma rays
λ	1500 m	3×10^{-2} m	6×10^{-7} m	10^{-12} m
f	2×10^5 Hz	10^{10} Hz	5×10^{14} Hz	3×10^{20} Hz
E	10^{-28} J	7×10^{-24} J	3×10^{-19} J	2×10^{-13} J
	10^{-9} eV	4×10^{-5} eV	2 eV	10^6 eV

Table 1

Q7 Nuclei also have energy levels. It takes 2.2 MeV energy to break apart a deuteron (a neutron plus proton). What wavelength of radiation is needed to do this? Is your answer the smallest or the largest wavelength that will do?

Q8 The school 3 cm microwave apparatus has a power of about 10^{-3} watt. How many photons does it emit each second? each cycle of oscillation? (Velocity of microwaves $= 3 \times 10^8$ m s^{-1}.)

Q9 Your answer to question 8 may be 10^{20} photons per second. How much power would a gamma ray source deliver if it emitted 10^{20} photons each second? (Use the data in table 1.) A school gamma ray source does not burn a hole in its box, despite this calculation. Do its photons each have less energy?

Demonstration
10.3 Counting photons

If a Geiger counter is held near a source of gamma rays, the counter shows random individual counts, there being perhaps 10^3 counts per second at most. The answer to question 9 shows why this number must be fairly small, and the answer to question 8 shows why a similar experiment with microwaves which are also electromagnetic waves, will not show lumpy, quantum behaviour. Since the frequency of gamma rays is of the order of 10^{20} Hz, if there are 10^3 photons in a second, there is only one photon in every 10^{17} cycles. So the number of photons in a second is not the same as the number of cycles in a second.

Demonstration
10.3 Counting photons

> 130/6 gamma GM tube
> 130/3 GM tube holder
> 130/1 scaler
> 195/1 pure gamma source

Simply place the GM tube close to the gamma source, showing that the number of counts is small at large distances, rising to about 10^3 s^{-1} at small distances. This experiment is intended simply to suggest that gamma ray quanta are few, as they should be if they are large in size. Stronger conclusions cannot be drawn, **a** because the tube detects perhaps one in a hundred of the photons entering it, **b** because the 'lumpy' nature of the observations might just as well be explained by saying that the tube 'fires' when enough wave energy has been delivered.

See the *Appendix*, page 137, for an optional demonstration (10.10) of the Compton effect. This work can be done now if an extra double period or so of time can be spared. A very simple discussion of the relevance of the Compton effect to the existence of photons is given in this Appendix.

The emission of photons

The photo-electric effect suggests that when light energy arrives, it does so in parcels of size $E = hf$. We now consider whether a similar description will serve for the emission of light by an atom. In Unit 2, Part Five, 'Electrons and energy levels', experiments were described which suggested that atoms gain or lose energy only in lumps, jumping from one level to another. In particular, the energy levels of mercury atoms were found.

Q10 In the electron bombardment experiments mentioned above, were quanta of light used to give evidence for the existence of energy levels? How was the evidence obtained?

Demonstration
10.4 The spectrum of mercury vapour

In Unit 5, *Atomic structure*, the spectrum of mercury was examined. Mercury atoms in a vapour, like other isolated atoms, emit light only at certain sharp wavelengths. If light from a slit is formed into a spectrum, the spectrum is composed of narrow lines. Using a grating, the wavelength of any line can be found from the angle at which it is formed. What lines might be expected in the mercury spectrum? The electron bombardment experiments with mercury vapour suggested that mercury atoms could accept energy in lumps of size 4.90 electronvolts, or 7.84×10^{-19} J, as well as in lumps of a number of other sizes. If mercury atoms emit photons with this energy, the frequency will be 11.8×10^{14} Hz, dividing the photon energy by Planck's constant h. The wavelength will be 2.53×10^{-7} m, dividing the velocity of light by the frequency. Such 'light' is in the ultra-violet part of the spectrum. Indeed, its existence is a reason why mercury lamps are used for sterilizing things, since the ultra-violet light can destroy bacteria. The ultra-violet line at wavelength 2.53×10^{-7} m can be detected in light from mercury vapour.

Demonstration
10.4 The spectrum of mercury vapour
(see experiment 5.18)

1071	mercury discharge lamp	
1073	concave reflection grating	
	screen with slit (see below)	
1053	strip of fluorescent paper, 20 mm wide, 0.5 m long, green	
503–6	retort stand base, rod, boss, and clamp	
1056	a little mercury in a polythene bottle	
1055	microscope slide	
191/2	fine grating	

Safety This experiment involves ultra-violet light and mercury vapour: both are potentially dangerous. Please observe the safety precautions in the following instructions.

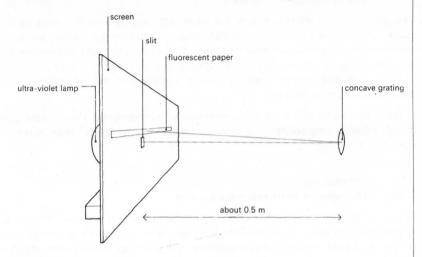

Figure 5
Production of mercury spectrum using a reflection grating.

Figure 5 shows a suitable arrangement. A screen, 0.3 m high and 0.6 m wide, is placed in front of the mercury discharge lamp, with a slit 1 mm wide opposite the aperture in the lamp casing. A strip of green fluorescent paper is pinned across the screen above the slit, on top of white, non-fluorescent paper. *The screen must be large enough to protect the class from stray ultra-violet light, and no student should look directly at the lamp.*

Fix the grating at a distance from the screen equal to its radius of curvature (about 0.5 m), so as to cast a spectrum back on the screen, with the zero order image of the slit in focus and just above the slit. Tilt the grating so that the diffracted orders lie over the horizontal strip of fluorescent paper, but fall partly on the white paper, as in figure 6. Any ultra-violet lines appear only on the fluorescent paper, visible lines being seen on both. Run the lamp at a low level at this stage.

Put a microscope slide over the slit: the ultra-violet lines vanish. *Gently* squeeze a polythene bottle containing *a few drops* of mercury so that the vapour comes out just in front of the grating. The ultra-violet lines fade or vanish for a moment. *Close the bottle immediately.* The experiment may be used in passing to illustrate the existence of a vapour, which is very poisonous, even above cold mercury. *Do not warm the mercury in an attempt to get more vapour.*

Measure the distances between the zero order line and the first order green line, and the *second order* ultra-violet line near the green line. The wavelength of the ultra-violet line can be inferred from its position near the green line, either by using the grating spacing, or, more simply, by assuming the wavelength of the green line (5.46×10^{-7} m).

The class may use the fine transmission gratings to observe the visible spectrum of mercury street lamps, and of other sources.

The presence of ultra-violet lines and their wavelength

If the spectrum of mercury vapour is formed by a diffraction grating and is cast onto both fluorescent paper and white paper, ultra-violet lines can be detected as glowing lines on the fluorescent paper only, whilst visible lines show up on both kinds of paper. Figure 6 shows the effect.

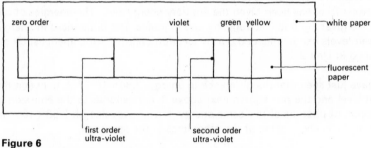

Figure 6
Spectrum of mercury using fluorescent paper to detect ultra-violet lines.

It is possible to confirm that the lines on the fluorescent paper are ultra-violet by holding a piece of glass over the source; then, only these lines vanish.

If cold mercury vapour is puffed into the air in front of the grating, so that the light has to pass twice through the vapour, both the ultra-violet lines fade or vanish.

It seems probable from this evidence that the two ultra-violet lines are the first and second order spectra of the same wavelength. It also seems likely that light of this wavelength corresponds to a jump between energy levels, one of which is the lowest possible level. This is because cold mercury vapour, most of whose atoms will be in the lowest level, absorbs the radiation strongly; presumably it does so as these atoms jump up to the level 4.9 electronvolts above the lowest level, taking the necessary energy from the radiation.

The measured wavelength of the ultra-violet light should correspond closely with the predicted wavelength, 2.53×10^{-7} m, calculated from the energy level difference 4.9 electronvolts.

Spectral lines and energy levels

Table 2 gives the wavelengths, frequencies, and photon energies of some of the lines in the mercury vapour spectrum.

Colour	Wavelength λ/m	Frequency f/Hz	Photon energy hf/J
yellow	5.79×10^{-7}	5.18×10^{14}	3.42×10^{-19}
green	5.46×10^{-7}	5.50×10^{14}	3.64×10^{-19}
violet	4.35×10^{-7}	6.90×10^{14}	4.56×10^{-19}
ultra-violet	2.53×10^{-7}	11.80×10^{14}	7.84×10^{-19}

Table 2

Figure 7 shows some of the levels in the mercury atom's ladder of energy levels. The lowest level has been given the arbitrary energy zero. The energies of other levels are given both in electronvolts and in joules. The differences in energies between levels can be mapped out by electron collision experiments such as those described in Unit 2.

You have just seen that the difference in energy, 7.84×10^{-19} J, between the lowest level and the one shown next above it, corresponds to the emission or absorption of photons of this same energy, having wavelength 2.53×10^{-7} m. Question 11 is about some of the other lines in the spectrum.

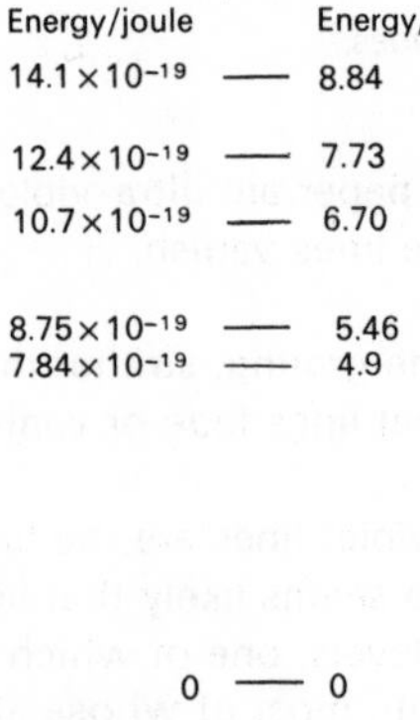

Energy/joule	Energy/eV
14.1×10^{-19} ——	8.84
12.4×10^{-19} ——	7.73
10.7×10^{-19} ——	6.70
8.75×10^{-19} ——	5.46
7.84×10^{-19} ——	4.9
0 ——	0

Figure 7
Some energy levels of mercury.

Q11a The yellow line corresponds to a jump starting at the highest level shown. Down to which one?

   b The green and violet lines both come from jumps down from the level at 12.4×10^{-19} J. Which *must* be the bigger jump?

   c There is a spectral line corresponding to a jump from the level at 14.1×10^{-19} J to the level at 7.84×10^{-19} J. Is the line visible?

Notes for teachers

1 We choose mercury for the above discussion so that students may see how energy levels and spectral lines are linked, in a case where previous work indicates a source of knowledge of energy level differences independent of spectral evidence. The previous, empirical study of energy levels was in Unit 2.

2 Electrical measurements of energy levels are none too precise, and a level difference given to three or more significant figures almost certainly comes from spectral evidence.

3 Not all the mercury levels are shown in figure 7. Nor do all possible transitions occur: some are forbidden by selection rules.

4 A very good display page on the analysis of the mercury spectrum appears in PSSC *Physics*, second edition, page 644, or in PSSC *College physics*, page 630.

Summary: the evidence from spectra

Although it is hard to measure energy levels accurately by electron collision experiments, it can be done. The differences E between these levels agree with the energies calculated from $E = hf$, using the frequencies f of the spectral lines that are observed coming from atoms. Light seems to be emitted from atoms just as if one photon of energy $E = hf$ arises from a jump between levels with an energy difference E. The value of h which decides photon sizes in the photo-electric effect also decides photon sizes and frequencies in spectra.

Q12 Using $E = hf$, one can work out energy levels *from* the frequencies of spectral lines, and doing it this way is more accurate than using collisions. What would be wrong with quoting energy levels worked out from spectral frequencies for the analysis of a spectrum as given above in question 11?

Q13 The quantity $h = 6.6 \times 10^{-34}$ J s has now appeared to work in two different situations. Would you think it fair to claim h as a universal constant?

Mapping energy levels from spectra

We have seen with the mercury spectrum how, if the energy levels are known, possible spectral lines can be predicted. Using this idea the other way round, it is possible to map energy levels using spectral evidence. We shall now map out the energy levels of hydrogen atoms. These are going to be important, because we shall develop a theory which predicts and explains the energy levels of simple atoms. This is the revolutionary theory called wave mechanics or quantum theory, which this work is all about. The analysis of the hydrogen spectrum is set out as a series of questions (numbers 14 to 20).

The energy levels of the hydrogen atom

Experiment
10.5 The hydrogen spectrum

Look at a hydrogen discharge tube through a diffraction grating or a direct vision spectroscope. You should see a number of bright lines in the visible region, the wavelengths of which can be measured using the grating formula $n\lambda = d \sin\theta$. You need not measure them. It is possible to photograph the spectrum with a camera focused on the tube, with a grating over the camera lens.

Experiment
10.5 The hydrogen spectrum

191/2	fine grating
193/2	hydrogen spectrum tube
194	holder for spectrum tubes
14	e.h.t. power supply
1000	leads

Run the discharge tube from the e.h.t. supply. Look at it through the grating, held near the eye with its rulings parallel to the tube.

Not all hydrogen tubes give the atomic hydrogen line spectrum. The trouble seems to be due to age. The demountable discharge tube (item 144) can be filled with hydrogen from a balloon, which has been filled from a hydrogen cylinder. The tube is then pumped out (vacuum pump, item 13) until the spectrum appears (with the e.h.t. supply connected).

For a bright spectrum, the 50 MΩ resistor in the e.h.t. supply should not be in circuit.

Figure 8 shows a photograph of the hydrogen spectrum, with a scale of wavelengths in units of 10^{-8} metre. The visible region stops at about $\lambda = 4 \times 10^{-7}$ m, in the middle of the photograph, and the lines to the left of that are in the invisible ultra-violet, which of course can be photographed. It is the brighter (thick) lines that are from hydrogen atoms. Some of the others come from other atoms or molecules present in the discharge tube.

Figure 8
The hydrogen spectrum.

Table 3 gives wavelengths and frequencies for the hydrogen spectrum, divided into three groups. It is the middle, Balmer series of lines that shows in the photograph.

Lyman series		Balmer series		Paschen series	
wavelength /10^{-7} m	frequency /10^{14} Hz	wavelength /10^{-7} m	frequency /10^{14} Hz	wavelength /10^{-7} m	frequency /10^{14} Hz
1.2157	24.659	6.5647	4.5665	18.756	1.5983
1.0257	29.226	4.8626	6.1649	12.822	2.3380
0.9725	30.824	4.3416	6.9044	10.941	2.7399
0.9497	31.564	4.1029	7.3064	10.052	2.9822
0.9378	31.966	3.9712	7.5487	9.5484	3.1395
0.9307	32.208	3.8901	7.7060		
0.9262	32.365				
....	....				
....	....				

Limit 32.881×10^{14} Hz

Table 3
The hydrogen spectrum.

There are other high frequency lines in the Lyman series but as the frequencies get larger they also get closer and closer together and the series seems to converge to the limiting value quoted in table 3.

Q14 Locate on the photograph in figure 8 the Balmer line of wavelength 6.56×10^{-7} m. Is the last line tabulated (at 3.89×10^{-7} m) observable? Are there more lines of still shorter wavelength?

Q15 The lines in the Lyman series are of shorter wavelength and larger frequency, all in the ultra-violet. The first two lines are at frequencies

24.659×10^{14} Hz
29.226×10^{14} Hz.

The first Balmer line is at a frequency of:

4.5665×10^{14} Hz.

Can you spot a connection between these three frequencies?

Q16 Suppose an atom has three energy levels, with levels at energies E_1, E_2 above the lowest level (figure 9). Spectral lines of frequency f_1, f_2 may appear, where

$E_1 = hf_1$
$E_2 = hf_2$.

What other spectral line frequency is also likely? Discuss the connection with question 15.

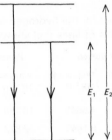

Figure 9

Q17 Suppose an atom has four energy levels, with one level of much lower energy than the others (as in figure 10). Then three of the spectral lines (A, B, C) will be of higher frequency (large energy changes) than the two others (D, E). What does this idea suggest about a possible relationship between the seven Lyman frequencies and the six Balmer frequencies given in table 3?

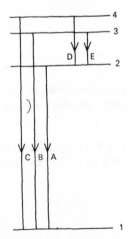

Figure 10

When the Lyman and Balmer series are compared, the ideas suggested by questions 15, 16, and 17 can be put together to give a simple scheme of energy levels that might explain all the frequencies. The same analysis can be used again when the Balmer and Paschen series are compared. We start by assuming that the Lyman series is a set of frequencies like A B C, figure 10, coming from energy differences all involving one lowest level, like level 1 of figure 10. Then the Lyman frequencies, all plotted on one vertical scale, give a set of possible energy levels. The Balmer and Paschen series are plotted on the same vertical scale, traced on slips of paper, and slid up alongside some Lyman lines. Figure 11 shows the result.

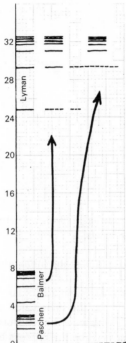

Figure 11
Analysis of the hydrogen spectrum.

Q18 What do you notice about the positions of the shifted frequencies?

Q19 Calculate the energies of photons corresponding to the first two Lyman frequencies,
$$24.659 \times 10^{14} \text{ Hz}$$
$$29.226 \times 10^{14} \text{ Hz}.$$

Q20 Write down, without using $E = hf$, the photon energy of the first Balmer frequency, $f = 4.566 \times 10^{14}$ Hz.

In table 4, the energy levels of hydrogen that will explain the observed frequencies have been written out. You have, in question 19, calculated the first two. The first and lowest level, with index number $n = 1$, has arbitrarily been given zero energy. The observed frequencies can only tell us about differences in energy between levels so that the choice of a zero is arbitrary, like deciding to measure heights from sea level as zero.

Energy/J	n (index number of level)
0	1
16.30×10^{-19}	2
19.35×10^{-19}	3
20.40×10^{-19}	4
20.80×10^{-19}	5
21.10×10^{-19}	6
21.30×10^{-19}	7
21.40×10^{-19}	8
etc.	
Limit 21.80×10^{-19}	$n = \infty$

Table 4
Energy levels of hydrogen.

Every frequency f in the observed spectrum has a photon energy hf that is equal to the difference between one pair of these levels.

Figure 12 shows the energy levels plotted against the index numbers n.

The energies rise towards a limit, between 21.5 and 22.0×10^{-19} J. The accepted value is 21.8×10^{-19} J. This 'limit energy' has the same value as the ionization energy of hydrogen (13.6 electronvolts), which can be measured independently by electron collision experiments. Ionization must be the process of lifting an electron from level 1 to the limit of the series of levels.

The electron in the hydrogen atom seems always to have one or other of a series of definite energies, which get closer and closer together until, at 21.8×10^{-19} J, the levels merge and the electron has escaped.

From similar evidence from spectra or electron collisions, the energy levels of other atoms may be determined. All have this feature of levels reaching up to a limit beyond which the atom is ionized.

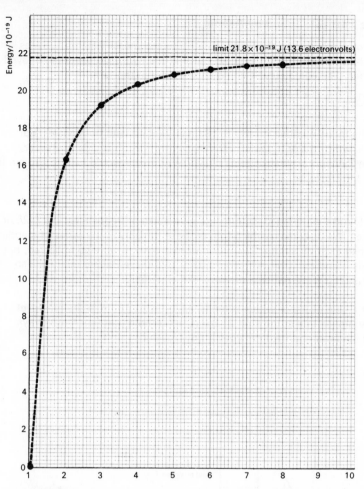

Figure 12

Index number *n* for each level

Energy levels of hydrogen against number *n* attached to each level.

If, as in table 4, the energy of level 1 is called zero, then an electron which has escaped from the atom will have 21.8×10^{-19} J more energy than this (if it only just had enough energy to get out and has no energy left over for kinetic energy). It is often convenient instead to choose as zero the energy of a free electron – one not trapped in an atom. If this is done, then we say that an electron in level 1 is 21.8×10^{-19} J *below* that of the free electron, and we might say that E_1 is *minus* 21.8×10^{-19} J.

The $1/n^2$ rule found by Balmer

In 1885, following hot upon the first accurate spectral measurements, a Swiss physics teacher, Johann Balmer, pointed out that the hydrogen spectrum obeyed a remarkable rule. The energy levels could each be put in the form

$$-\frac{21.8 \times 10^{-19}}{n^2},$$

where n is the index number in table 4. (Balmer worked with frequencies, not energy levels, which made it harder.) The discovery was no accident: Balmer believed, like Pythagoras, that patterns of whole numbers would help to explain the mysteries of the Universe.

Pythagoras found that stringed instruments give notes of frequencies like f, $2f$, $3f$, etc. in a series. We now realize the origin of these integers in the series of standing waves that can exist on strings. The music of hydrogen is more complicated, but we now think — and this Unit will show how — that these Balmer integers also arise from standing wave patterns of wave-like electrons.

Q21 Cut a strip of paper which extends, as in figure 13, from the first level (zero) to the broken line at the limit 21.8×10^{-19} J. Fold it in four lengthways. Between which level and the limit does it now reach?

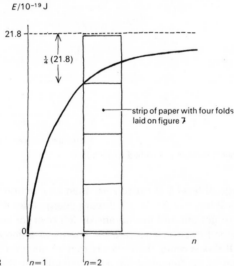

$E/10^{-19}$ J

21.8

$\frac{1}{4}(21.8)$

strip of paper with four folds laid on figure 7

0

n

Figure 13 $n=1$ $n=2$

Some open questions

Hydrogen atoms are about 0.5×10^{-10} metre in radius (Units 1 and 5 looked at the size of atoms), and each needs 13.6 electronvolts (21.8×10^{-19} J) energy to become ionized. Can these values be explained? Why do the energy levels follow a simple $1/n^2$ numerical law? Why are there energy levels anyway? These are some of the questions we shall try to answer in Part Three. Before that, we return to photons to puzzle a little more about what light is like.

Photons – waves and particles

'If one does not feel a little dizzy when discussing the implications of Planck's constant h it means that one does not know what one is talking about.'

Niels Bohr.

So far our discussion has concentrated on the particle-like aspect of light. But light has wave properties too. The discussion here will be helped if you see, or have seen two films: 'Photons' and 'Interference of photons'.

Note to teachers

See page 160 for details about these two PSSC films.

'Photons' tries to show that if a brief burst of light is made so faint that in one burst a sensitive photocell (photomultiplier) will emit no more than one electron, the wave prediction that it will be necessary to wait until the end of the burst until enough energy has been delivered is false. Electrons can come out whenever the photon happens to arrive, and one occasionally comes right at the start of the burst. The argument in the film is open to the criticism that unless it is shown that the energy delivered in a burst is really less than the 1 electronvolt or so needed to eject an electron, there could be plenty of wave energy available. If the ejection of an electron is just not very likely the same result is obtained.

'Interference of photons' is, for our purposes, much the more useful film. It shows the random, lumpy arrival of energy in an interference pattern, the chance of energy arriving being large where a wave would be large and small where waves would cancel. In this film, it is pointed out that the photomultiplier releases an electron from about one photon in a thousand, which exposes the problem raised above about 'Photons'.

Consider an example of wave behaviour that is easy to observe – the spectrum of a diffraction grating when light of a single wavelength is shone on it. (Figure 14.)

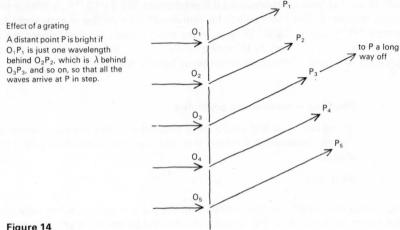

Effect of a grating

A distant point P is bright if O_1P_1 is just one wavelength behind O_2P_2, which is λ behind O_3P_3, and so on, so that all the waves arrive at P in step.

to P a long way off

Figure 14

What can we think about this if light is a stream of bullets? One particle can only go through one slit: how can the direction it takes on coming out be affected by the other slits which it hasn't gone through? But the pattern when all slits are open is very different from the pattern for only one slit. You should have seen the effect of changing the number of slits in Unit 8, *Electromagnetic waves*.

Perhaps it is something to do with the fact that in a light beam there are many bullets going through; maybe other bullets going through O_2, O_3, and other slits, affect one that goes through O_1, and together they give the diffraction pattern. This can be tested if we work with very feeble light. It can be made so feeble that photons go through one at a time: then they can't affect one another. In that case the argument that one particle can only go through one slit will still hold and the diffraction pattern should perhaps disappear for feeble light.

Your eye is a very sensitive photon detector, if it has had time to adapt to darkness. It is fairly easy to arrange, with a grating in front of your eye, that there is only one photon at a time between the grating and the retina, on which a diffraction pattern may be formed.

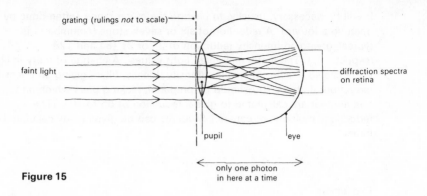

grating (rulings *not* to scale)

faint light

diffraction spectra on retina

pupil

eye

Figure 15

only one photon
in here at a time

Experiment
10.6 Interference of single photons

52 A	flashlamp bulb 1.25 V, 0.25 A
52 C	baseboard
52 D	spring connector with lampholder
52 B	U2 cell
1053	fogged photographic film
1053	cardboard slide mounts, 35 mm
191/1	coarse grating
1055	photographic exposure meter
	slide projector

Students look at a torch bulb, and observe the diffraction spectrum. Then slides containing fogged film are propped against the bulb, so as to reduce the intensity by a large known factor (see below). If this factor is large enough, students can calculate that the photons in flight to their eyes are an arm's length or more behind one another, so that they cross the grating and eye one at a time. At this intensity, in a well blacked out room, the bulb filament is still just visible, and the diffraction spectrum can still be seen. Students need to stand about half a metre from a lamp so one lamp and one set of filters can serve about four observers.

To make the fogged film, pull the film out of its cassette and expose it to daylight for a minute or so. The film can be developed in a tank or dish. Fixing and washing are advisable if the film is to be used in later years.

To calibrate the filters, put an exposure meter in the direct beam of a slide projector, and move it until it reads near maximum. Put a fogged film slide into the projector, and without moving the meter, take the new reading.

It will be necessary, usually, to change the meter range (often done by opening a louvre). A reduction of six or seven stops (*f*-numbers) is typical, giving an intensity reduction of 2^6 or 2^7 (64 and 128 respectively). The meter may read 'light values'. A change of unity in light value is also a factor of two in intensity. Ideally, filters giving an intensity reduction of about 100 should be prepared, making pairs which on top of one another are calculated to give a reduction of up to 10^4. (The reductions multiply, of course.) Students can be given ready calibrated filters.

Experiment
10.6 Interference of single photons

Look at a torch bulb through a diffraction grating. You should see a spectrum easily.

Q22 The bulb emits about 0.3 W in all (multiply current and p.d.) of which about 10^{-2} W is visible light, the rest being heat. About how many visible photons does it emit each second? ($f \approx 6 \times 10^{14}$ Hz, $h = 6.6 \times 10^{-34}$ J s.)

Q23 If your eye is about 0.3 m from the bulb, about one photon in 50 000 enters your eye (pupil area divided by total area of a sphere 0.3 m radius). About how many photons enter your eye in a second?

Q24 Light travels at 3×10^8 m s^{-1}. When one photon enters your eye, how far behind it is the next one that will enter, on average? (First work out what fraction of a second there is between photons.)

Q25 You should be given a pair of fogged film filters, that together reduce the intensity by up to 10^4 times, to prop up in front of the lamp. How 'far apart' are the few photons that now get through to your eye?

You should have found, in answering question 25, that the photons that will enter your eye are now up to 3 m 'apart' on average. As your eye is about $\frac{1}{10}$ this distance from the lamp, there is only one photon 'on the way' at any instant. (There are still 10^8 photons entering your eye each second, though.)
The photons now go through the grating singly and alone and travel to your retina with no others to 'interfere' with. On a simple particle picture, a particle photon obviously cannot go through more than one slit. But the grating spectrum will only be seen if something wavelike goes through *every* slit – the spectrum is explained by adding waves from many slits. Does the spectrum vanish, or not? This is the test.

If you look carefully, you will see that the pattern is still there. How *can* there be a diffraction pattern? Only rarely will two or more photons go through the grating and eye together. Yet the diffraction pattern is explained by saying that part of the light goes through every slit! Somehow a particle photon 'interferes with itself', as if something like a wave went through every slit. Such experiments have been done many times. The film 'Interference of photons' is one version. Another was made in 1909 by G. I. Taylor, who took diffraction photographs with light so feeble that his exposure time reached 3 months. Rumour has it that he went on holiday during the experiment.

We are back up against the fundamental worry about quantum ideas. A particle (photon) model is needed. When we take it seriously and look for the vanishing of wave effects when the radiation is feeble, we find that a wave model is still needed to explain the results. Neither model will do for all cases.

More needs for both models

Both models are needed to explain photo-electric experiments. The energy arrives in lumps $E = hf$, but how is f known? By measuring wavelength λ. How is λ known? By using a wave model to calculate $\lambda = d \sin \theta$ for the grating. Figure 16 shows how one experiment needs two models.

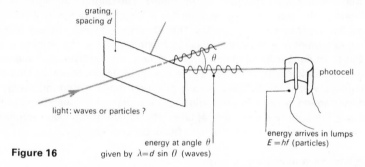

Figure 16

energy at angle θ given by $\lambda = d \sin \theta$ (waves)

Figure 17 shows the wavelength of X-rays being measured by a crystal, whose regularly spaced atoms act like a grating. Waves would be reflected strongly at angles given by the Bragg rule $\lambda = 2d \sin \theta$, and the X-rays are reflected at definite angles only. λ can be calculated. Yet the counter shows, as usual in an X-ray or gamma ray beam, irregular 'clicks' as photons arrive one by one. This experiment also needs both models.

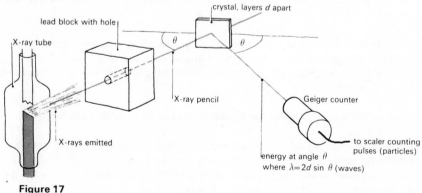

Figure 17

Chance and the arrival of photons

We now introduce an important new idea into the story: the idea of chance. Chance and randomness have appeared before in the course, mainly in Unit 5, *Atomic structure*, when discussing radioactive decay, and in Unit 9, *Change and chance,* where chance was the basis of the understanding of thermal equilibrium.

Chance enters the description of light in an attempt to make the wave and the particle models fit together in one important respect: in making them give the same answers for the rate of arrival of energy in a beam of light.

The answer from the particle model is simple enough. The amount of energy delivered every second by a beam of photons is the number of photons that arrive each second, multiplied by the energy of one photon, *hf*.

The answer from the wave model is a little subtler. The brighter the light, the bigger the amplitude of the wave, but the two are not in direct proportion. In Unit 6, *Electronics and reactive circuits*, you saw that the energy exchanged per second by an alternating current in a resistance was in proportion, not to the amplitude of the current, but to its square. Similarly, in Unit 4, *Waves and oscillations*, the energy stored by a harmonic oscillator varied as the square of its amplitude. In Unit 8, *Electromagnetic waves*, some reasons were given for thinking that the energy delivered by a sound wave is in proportion to the square of the amplitude of the wave motion. For light, the same rule applies. The square of the wave amplitude is in proportion to the rate at which the light beam delivers energy.

If particle and wave model are to agree,

number of photons arriving per second $\propto$ square of wave amplitude.

But the photons in an interference or diffraction pattern do not arrive in a steady, regular stream. The film 'Interference of photons', or experiments with X-rays detected by a GM counter, show that the photon energy parcels land at random, coming in quite irregularly. It isn't possible to predict where an individual photon will go, except that it will go rarely where the pattern is dark, and often where it is bright.

The arrival of photons is rather like spraying something with an aerosol paint spray. Suppose you point a can of spray paint at a screen, and give a short burst. (Figure 18 *a*.) A second burst (*b*) and a third larger one (*c*) will build up a pattern of paint drops.

A very long burst will cover the screen with paint to a varying thickness (*d*).

If the paint spray is replaced by a lamp, for which lenses or apertures gave a brightness variation the same as the paint density variation (*e*), then with the lamp turned low you would see photons arriving in the same random way as the paint drops, gradually building up the final intensity.

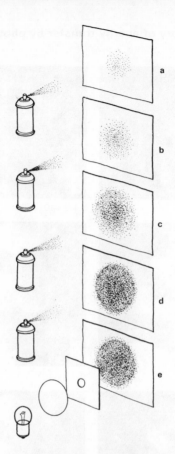

Figure 18

For the lamp and lens, wave theory can predict the amplitude at each place. The brightness is proportional to (amplitude)². The number of photons coming in to each place varies in the same way as (amplitude)² varies.

Putting together the models of photons-arriving-by-chance and the wave-amplitude-decided-by-interference, we have:

chance of a photon arriving $\propto$ (wave amplitude)².

The strange story of energy transfer by photons

No. of photons

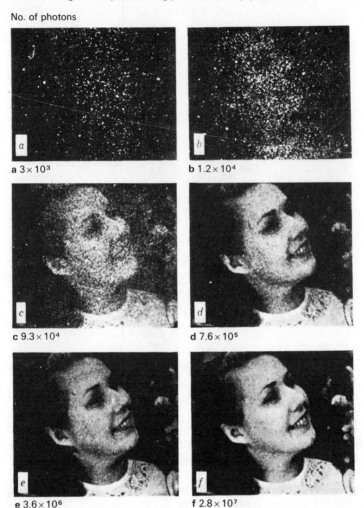

a 3×10^3

b 1.2×10^4

c 9.3×10^4

d 7.6×10^5

e 3.6×10^6

f 2.8×10^7

Figure 19

Series of photographs showing the quality of picture obtainable from various numbers of photons.
Photographs, Rose, A. (1957). Advances in biological and medical physics, *5, 211.*

Figure 19 comes from Rose, A. (1957) *Advances in biology and medical physics*, **5**, 211–242. We are grateful to an early draft of the M.I.T. *Introductory physics series,* by Professor A. P. French, for bringing these photographs to our attention.

Figure 19 vividly illustrates what abstract arguments about the chance arrival of photons mean in practice. The photographs were made to represent the quality of picture obtainable using dim light. When the light is dim, the picture breaks up into a number of randomly placed spots, just as if a number of lumps of light energy had been delivered to particular places.

It does seem, then, that when light spreads out and so becomes feebler, we must imagine the energy it carries parcelled up into quanta of definite size, which are more or less densely spread out in space. It is necessary to add that the place where the energy of a photon will be delivered cannot be predicted in advance, though many will in the end fall where the wave amplitude is large.

Time effects

The fact that there is no detectable delay in the emission of photo-electrons, even in dim light, helps to confirm the story. In one experiment (Elster, J., and Geitel, H., 1912, *Phys. Zeits.* **13**, 468–476), light of intensity less than 10^{-10} W m^{-2} produced electrons with energy of the order 10^{-19} J, with no detectable delay. On a wave model, a wave will deliver energy into an area of the order of the square of its wavelength; certainly less than 10^{-12} m^2 in this instance (wavelength 5×10^{-7} m). Energy was therefore obtainable from the wave by an electron no faster than 10^{-22} J s^{-1}. To obtain 10^{-19} J, it would be necessary to wait 1000 seconds: over a quarter of an hour. Any one such area, on a photon picture, must wait an average of a quarter of an hour between photons, but in a surface of several square centimetres, some such areas will receive photons with as little delay as one pleases, and emission starts at once. On a wave model, all areas must wait together and no electron can emerge for a quarter of an hour.

To see how strange all this is, consider the following peculiar story.

A harbour master is told that there has been an earthquake out at sea, and a large wave is spreading out from it. He works out from the speed of sea waves that the wave can be expected at noon, but he also calculates that, though the wave was large near the source, because it is spreading out it will be less than half a metre high when it reaches his harbour. So he expects all the boats in the harbour to rise and fall gently. At noon, he watches the boats. Nothing happens. Then suddenly, one boat shoots ten metres into the air, while the rest stay quite still. Then, as though someone were throwing dice to pick on which boat will be affected, other boats, quite at random, shoot up suddenly. But where he had expected all the boats to rise a little, he sees many fewer boats shoot up much more.

This is how sea wave energy would arrive if it behaved as light does.

How light behaves – a summary

Light delivers its energy in lumps or photons, of size $E = hf$.

A bright beam contains many such photons, a feeble beam few. High frequency radiation has bigger photons, and thus, has fewer of them for a given power. The photons travel at 3×10^8 m s^{-1}.

If the light shines on a grating, or a pair of slits, energy still turns up at a detector in lumps. But the lumps do not turn up evenly spread out, as they do if there is no grating. Many arrive at some places, few at others. They come in no predictable order, but they do pile up into a pattern. And that pattern is the pattern wave energy would arrive in if the wave had gone through *all* the slits.

If you cover up some slits, the photons arrive in a new pattern: the one for waves going through all those slits that are still left open. This effect has been seen in Unit 8, with gratings having different numbers of slits.

Photons are only observed when the light reaches a detector: because of this you might argue that questions about what photons do *en route* have no meaning. However, if you want to say what happens to a photon *en route* you have to say that it goes through the grating in one of many possible ways, the behaviour of many photons being such that there is a good chance of them landing in a wave maximum and a small chance of them landing in a wave minimum. The chances are just right for many photons to build up exactly the pattern which the wave theory predicts.

How does a photon decide where to go? It doesn't; one goes one way, another goes another, and they do these things just often enough to build up the right wave pattern.

Which slit did each photon go through? We can't tell.

Is light really photons? No, how could the slits a photon didn't go through affect its path?

Is light really waves? No, how could feeble waves deliver a bunch of energy before enough wave energy had arrived?

What is light? Light.

How does light behave? As we said.

Why does it behave so? No one knows.

> *No one knows?* On the last point, one might want to say, 'Light is an
> oscillating system; oscillators are quantized, so that is why light behaves
> as it does'. This leaves the question, 'Why are oscillators quantized?'.
> 'The rules say so.' 'Why are those the rules?' 'No one knows.'

Nobody likes it – but that's how it is

Nobody likes this strange mixture of two models when they first meet it. But then
Newton's Laws, especially Law I, seem strange at first too, and even more so do
ideas about the Earth being round with people 'upside down' on the other side.
The idea of Copernicus that the Earth travels round the Sun seemed hopelessly
implausible – even unintelligible – to many people. *Of course* the Earth was sitting
in the middle of the Universe, they thought. *Of course* light must be one thing or
the other, you may say. You would not be alone in feeling uneasy. Here are some
things that physicists and teachers have said about the quantum puzzle.

Project Physics, Unit 5, says:

> 'No one was prepared to find that both wave and particle descriptions
> could apply to light. But this dualism cannot be wished away, because
> it is based on experimental results.'

Sir William Bragg said:

> 'On Mondays, Wednesdays, and Fridays we adopt the one hypothesis, on
> Tuesdays, Thursdays, and Saturdays, the other.'

(But it is worse than that. We adopt both all week, including Sundays.)

Einstein was quite open about his doubts. In a letter to Born (1926) he says:

> 'The quantum mechanics is very imposing. But an inner voice tells me that
> it is still not the final truth. The theory yields much, but it hardly brings us
> nearer to the secret of the Old One. In any case, I am convinced that He
> does not play dice.'

PSSC *Physics* says:

> 'The study of the photon was the hard school in which physicists became
> more sophisticated in the ways of the world.'

Richard Feynman is one of the present-day research physicists who have learned to live with the problem. He works in theoretical quantum mechanics, and accepting the conflict is the only way he and others have found to make progress.

In *The Feynman lectures on physics*, Volume I, Chapter 37, he says:

> 'Things on a very small scale behave like nothing that you have any direct experience about. They do not behave like waves, they do not behave like particles, they do not behave like clouds, or billiard balls, or weights on springs, or like anything that you have ever seen.

> 'Newton thought that light was made up of particles, but then it was discovered . . . that it behaves like a wave. Later, however, . . . it was found that light did indeed sometimes behave like a particle. . . . Now we have given up. We say, "It is like *neither*".

> 'Because atomic behaviour is so unlike ordinary experience, it is very difficult to get used to and it appears peculiar and mysterious to everyone, both to the novice and the experienced physicist. Even the experts do not understand it the way they would like to, and it is perfectly reasonable that they should not, because all of direct human experience and of human intuition applies to large objects. We know how large objects will act, but things on a small scale just do not act that way.'

About the basic idea, bullets arriving by chance, in large numbers where a wave would arrive in large quantity, Feynman says:

> 'One might still like to ask: "How does it work? What is the machinery behind the law?" No one has found any machinery behind the law. No one can "explain" any more than we have just "explained". No one will give you any deeper representation [model] of the situation.'

It would not be surprising if by now you are feeling as Alice felt in the looking-glass world:

> 'Alice laughed. "There's no use trying," she said: "one *can't* believe impossible things."
> ' "I daresay you haven't had much practice," said the Queen. "When I was your age, I always did it for half-an-hour a day. Why, sometimes I've believed as many as six impossible things before breakfast." . . .'

Lewis Carroll, Through the looking-glass.

In Part Two you will get some more practice.

Part Two

Electrons

... For I neither conclude from one single Experiment, nor are the Experiments I make use of, all made upon one Subject: Nor wrest I any Experiment to make it quadrare [square] with any preconceiv'd Notion. But on the contrary, I endeavour to be conversant in all kinds of Experiments, and all and everyone of those Trials, I make the standards (as I may say) or Touchstones by which I try my former Notions. ...

Robert Hooke 1661.

'At this moment the King, who had been for some time busily writing in his notebook, called out "Silence!" and read out from his book, "Rule Forty-two. *All persons more than a mile high to leave the court."*
Everybody looked at Alice.
"I'm not a mile high," said Alice.
"You are," said the King.
"Nearly two miles high," added the Queen.
"Well, I shan't go, at any rate," said Alice: "besides, that's not a regular rule: you invented it just now."
"It's the oldest rule in the book," said the King.
"Then it ought to be Number One," said Alice.
The King turned pale, and shut his notebook hastily.
"Consider your verdict," he said to the jury, in a low trembling voice.

Lewis Carroll, Alice's adventures in Wonderland.

The wave properties of X-ray photons are widely used to obtain information about the arrangement of atoms in solids, using the diffraction patterns produced by regularly arranged atoms, which behave like three-dimensional diffraction gratings.

Figure 20 *a* is an example: an X-ray diffraction photograph of a polythene sample. Figure 20 *b* is a diffraction photograph of a rubber sample, but it was taken with a beam of electrons, not a beam of X-rays. *Electrons also have wave properties.*

Figure 20
a X-ray diffraction – polythene. *Photograph, Imperial Chemical Industries Ltd., Plastics Division.*
b Electron diffraction – stretched rubber. *Photograph, Professor E. H. Andrews.*

In Part One, the strange wave-and-particle behaviour of photons was described. The behaviour of photons may seem to you very peculiar, but there is one comfort: electrons behave in just the same way. All the interference and diffraction experiments that are possible with light can be duplicated with electrons, though the wavelength for electrons is usually very small.

Slides and photographs

Figures 20 *a* and 20 *b* come from Unit 1, and are slides 1.6 and 1.5 respectively. Slide 1.4 is another electron diffraction photograph, while slides 1.7, 1.8, and 1.9 are more X-ray photographs.

See also Plate III (b) and (c) in Born, M., *The restless Universe*, for another pair of X-ray and electron diffraction photographs.

Rogers, E. M., *Physics for the inquiring mind*, page 741, gives a pair of two-slit interference patterns, one for light and one for electrons.

PSSC *Physics*, second edition, page 627, gives a pair of photographs of diffraction at a straight edge.

Figures 21 and 22 show interference effects for X-rays and electrons respectively. Figure 21 shows the diffraction of X-rays produced by narrow wires of width 0.0436 mm, 0.0379 mm, 0.0188 mm (from Kellstrom *Nova acta Regiae. societatis scientiarum upsaliensis* Series **IV**, **8**, 5, page 61).

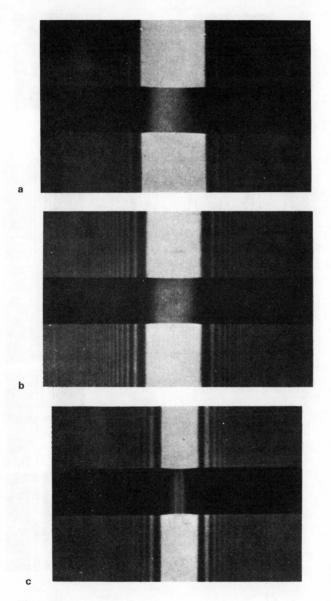

Figure 21
Diffraction of X-rays by narrow wires.

The top two photographs in figure 22 (from Jonsson, C., 1961, *Zeitschrift für Physik* **161**, 454) show electron diffraction at a single slit and at double slits. The pictures below show diffraction at three slits with theoretical intensity curves.

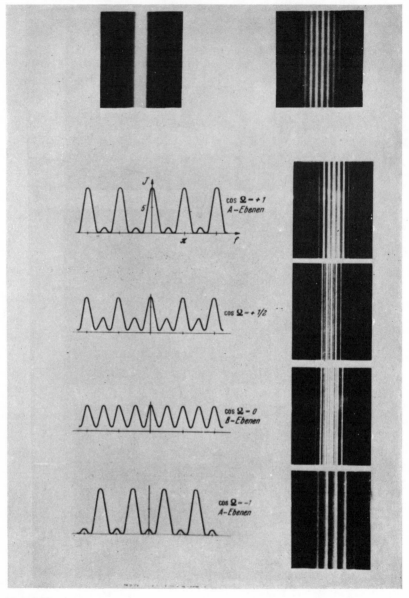

Figure 22
Diffraction of electrons at slits.

The wave behaviour of electrons is of practical as well as of deep theoretical importance. Electron diffraction is widely used in the study of the structures of materials.

Demonstration
10.7 Electron diffraction

In the demonstration tube shown in figure 23, an electron beam is focused onto a fluorescent screen on the end of the tube. The beam passes through a target made of graphite. (Graphite has the advantage that it does not melt or break up when heated by the electron beam.)

Figure 23
Electron diffraction tube.
Photograph, Teltron Ltd.

Q1 Why does the electron beam heat the target? Where does the energy come from?

The screen shows two (or more) rings, which we shall argue are a diffraction pattern somewhat like the ring patterns obtained with X-rays when diffracted by polycrystalline materials.

Demonstration
10.7 Electron diffraction

197	electron diffraction tube
14	e.h.t. power supply
27	transformer
50/1	cylindrical magnet

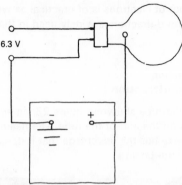

Figure 24
Circuit for electron diffraction tube.

The anode at the side of the tube is connected to the e.h.t. positive terminal, not using the 50 MΩ resistor. The negative terminal is earthed and connected to one of the filament sockets in the tube base. The filament requires 6.3 V. Two rings should be visible at voltages between 3 kV and 5 kV. As the voltage is raised the rings shrink in size, and become brighter. The ring diameter may be measured with a rule marked in millimetres.

A magnet placed near the neck of the tube will bend the electron beam and shift the whole pattern sideways.

At high voltages, the rings are small. As the voltage is lowered, the rings become larger.

Q2 In optical diffraction by a slit, say, does red light produce a broader, or a narrower pattern than blue light?

Q3 If experiment 10.7 really involves diffraction of electrons by a 'grating' of regularly placed atoms, how would the wavelength have to change to obtain an increase in the ring diameter, corresponding to an increase in the angle of diffraction?

Q4 The energy carried by the bombarding electrons heats the graphite target. What effect would an expansion of the target have on the ring diameter, if the effect were large enough to be noticeable (it is not)?

Q5 If the voltage on the anode is reduced, are the electrons in the beam travelling faster, more slowly, or at the same speed as before?

Q6 Does the behaviour of the rings when the voltage is varied suggest that slow electrons have the same, a larger, or a smaller wavelength than fast electrons?

If the phenomenon is diffraction, it seems that fast electrons have small wavelengths. Before we draw this conclusion, we examine a little more closely whether it is reasonable to suppose that the effect is due to diffraction.

Diffraction by graphite

The process used to deposit carbon atoms in a thin film on the target of the tube suggested, produces graphite in a special form. Layers of hexagons of carbon atoms, as shown in figure 25, are deposited parallel to the target, and perpendicular to the electron beam. Unlike figure 25, the layers are not quite perfect (some hexagons being deformed and having missing atoms), and the regions of approximately regular arrangement are not very big. Nor are successive layers, laid on top of one another, laid down in the fixed orientation in relation to one another which would be obtained in a true graphite structure.

A rough picture of the state of the target material may be obtained by imagining small platelets each containing a single layer of atoms arranged in some approximation to figure 25, but with the platelets laid down beside and on top of one another in a random fashion, rather like a pack of playing cards spread out in a jumble on a table.

Diffraction from such a material is *not* three-dimensional Bragg diffraction. Each small ordered layer acts like a two-dimensional diffraction grating, the net effect being the combined effect of many such gratings all in one plane but orientated at every possible angle in that plane.

A full treatment of two-dimensional diffraction is not simple. In what follows, we have treated a two-dimensional array of atoms as if parallel rows of atoms behave like parallel slits in an ordinary grating. Such a treatment is only approximate, but it happens that the system under discussion has too poor a resolution for any difference to be detected.

The structure of atomic layers in graphite is known, from X-ray diffraction. The carbon atoms form up in arrays of hexagons, as shown in figure 25. If you hold this figure at eye level and look across it, you should see rows of parallel lines of atoms. If you turn the page, different sets of lines will spring into prominence. We shall suppose (as is roughly true) that such a set of rows of atoms scatters a wave in the same fashion as a set of parallel rulings on a grating. For such a grating, if the

Figure 25
Arrangement of carbon atoms in a graphite layer. (Atoms in the target of the electron diffraction tube are arranged rather less perfectly.)

spacing of lines is d, and the wave has wavelength λ, there will be a first order diffraction maximum at an angle θ, where

$$\lambda = d \sin \theta.$$

The diffraction effect of a single such layer of atoms can be imitated using light passing through a grid of regularly arranged holes or spots. Figure 25, reduced onto a 35 mm film negative, makes a suitable grid. Look through the grid at a torch bulb about two metres away, and you should see a pattern of bright diffraction spots. Rotate the grid in its own plane, and then the spot pattern also turns. Since the graphite in the electron diffraction tube contains many such grids of atoms, placed at every possible angle, the pattern of spots is blurred out into several rings (usually two). If the optical grid is spun rapidly round, it too gives a ring pattern.

Preparation of optical grids

A set of grids can easily be made by photographing figure 25 on many frames of a roll of 35 mm black and white film, using the negatives as grids of 'holes' in a dark background.

Photograph the page at a distance of about one metre, so that the image of the page has linear dimensions about one-third that of the field of view. For good contrast, over- rather than underexpose. The negatives can be mounted in cardboard slide mounts, with the unwanted area masked by opaque adhesive tape.

A 2.5 V torch bulb, viewed at a distance of about two metres, with the grid held over the eye, makes a suitable object.

Q7 Using $\lambda = d \sin \theta$, and supposing that the two rings visible in the electron diffraction experiment do come from diffraction by rows of atoms with spacings d_1 and d_2, how ought the sines of the angles θ_1 and θ_2 to compare? Will their ratio depend on the wavelength?

Figure 27 (page 53) shows the diffraction angle θ and the ring diameter D. For each ring, D will be approximately proportional to $\sin \theta$. Therefore, if $\sin \theta_1 / \sin \theta_2$ is a constant ratio whatever the wavelength, the ratio D_1 / D_2 will also be constant. We saw before that the wavelength seems to change with the voltage. Thus, if the phenomenon is electron diffraction, the ratio D_1 / D_2 ought to stay the same if the tube voltage is varied. For the tube suggested, a range of 3 kV to 5 kV is suitable. Table 5 gives some sample results.

Electron gun p.d./V	D_1/mm	D_2/mm	D_2/D_1
5000	26	45	1.73
4000	28.5	49.5	1.74
3000	34	56	1.65
		Average	1.71

Table 5
Diffraction ring diameters.

The constancy of the ratio D_1/D_2 is consistent with the diffraction explanation of the rings, and its value gives information about the relative spacings of the rows of atoms responsible.

Q8 If the larger ring comes from diffraction by rows a distance d apart, does the smaller ring come from rows with spacing $1.7d$, or $d/1.7$?

Figure 26 indicates two sets of rows which could be responsible for the two rings. Because the hexagons of carbon atoms have sides 1.42×10^{-10} m long, the vertical lines show rows of atoms $\frac{\sqrt{3}}{2}(1.42 \times 10^{-10})$ m apart, while the horizontal lines show rows of atoms $\frac{3}{2}(1.42 \times 10^{-10})$ m apart. See figure 26 b for the geometry involved.

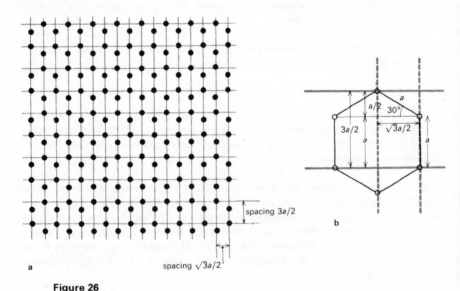

Figure 26
a Two row spacings in a graphite layer.
b Geometry of row spacings.

Q9 What is the ratio of the spacing of the two sets of rows shown in figure 26?

Q10 Does this ratio agree with the experimental results for the ratio of the two ring diameters?

The above arguments do not prove that the rows of atoms in figure 26 are the rows responsible, but the pattern of rings on the screen is consistent with what would be obtained by diffraction from a graphite structure.

Wavelength and energy or momentum of electrons

The p.d. V indicates the energy of the electrons, which rises as λ falls. One might suppose that (energy) $\times$ (wavelength) might be constant. At the time, about 1927, when electron diffraction was discovered in America by Davisson and Germer, and in England by G. P. Thomson, physicists knew of a speculation by the Frenchman, Louis de Broglie, that particles might be associated with waves. De Broglie based his ideas on similarities between some theories about light and theories of mechanics and had predicted that *momentum* multiplied by wavelength would be constant.

Momentum $mv \propto 1/\lambda.$

Q11 If the accelerating p.d. is V, will the velocity v of the electrons be proportional to V, $1/V$, $\sqrt{V}$, $1/\sqrt{V}$?

Thus to test de Broglie's idea, that $v \propto 1/\lambda$, calculate $D\sqrt{V}$ from your measurements and see if it is constant. (D is the ring diameter, V the gun voltage.)

Table 6 gives some results obtained by G. P. Thomson, taken from his 1928 paper describing his experiments on electron diffraction. They are for an aluminium target. You could test whether $D\sqrt{V}$ is constant. Thomson's voltages were estimated from the size of a spark gap and are not highly accurate.

Date	V/volt	D/cm
October 7	17 500	3.10
October 10	30 500	2.45
October 7	31 800	2.32
October 7	40 000	2.12
October 7	44 000	2.08
October 7	48 600	1.90
October 11	48 600	1.98
October 12	56 500	1.83
October 12	56 500	1.80

Table 6
Diffraction results obtained by G. P. Thomson.

Planck's constant h again

The measurements made in the electron diffraction experiment enable us to find the constant in the relation

$$mv \propto \frac{1}{\lambda}.$$

De Broglie originally suggested that the relation should be

$$mv = \frac{h}{\lambda},$$

where h is Planck's constant, 6.6×10^{-34} J s, which was met before in connection with photons.

In one experiment with the electron diffraction tube, the larger ring diameter was 45 mm at a p.d. of 5000 V (you may prefer to substitute your own data). The spacing d in graphite for the larger ring (the smaller spacing) is $\frac{\sqrt{3}}{2}(1.42 \times 10^{-10})$ m or 1.23×10^{-10} m. The target was 135 mm from the fluorescent screen.

Q12 What is the angle θ in figure 27, in radians?

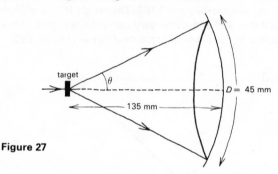

Figure 27

Q13 What is $\sin \theta$? (You may use an approximation.)

Q14 What is the wavelength λ, using $\lambda = d \sin \theta$?

Q15 The kinetic energy $\frac{1}{2}mv^2$ of an electron, charge q, accelerated through p.d. V, is qV. Write an equation in terms of q and V for its momentum mv.

Q16 For an electron, $q = 1.6 \times 10^{-19}$ C, $m = 9.1 \times 10^{-31}$ kg. Find the momentum for a p.d. of 5000 V.

Q17 Find the constant h in $mv = h/\lambda$.

Q18 Are the units of (momentum) $\times$ (wavelength) the same as those of (energy) (1/frequency)?

Q19 If the same value of h appears in both $E = hf$ and $mv = h/\lambda$, would that be a reason for thinking that h might be a universal constant?

Q20 The wavelength of 5000 volt electrons comes to about 0.2×10^{-10} m (see Q14). At what p.d. would accelerated electrons have a wavelength of 0.2×10^{-6} m? (Compare ultra-violet light.)

Other measurements of *h*

Figure 28 is a graph prepared by Davisson in 1928, collecting several people's results together. Wavelength λ is plotted against $1/\sqrt{V}$ where V is the accelerating p.d. You should have shown in answering question 15 that

$$mv = \sqrt{2mqV}.$$

Q21 Show that the slope of the graph is equal to $h/\sqrt{2mq}$. Find *h* from the slope (for this graph, V was measured in volts, λ in units of 10^{-10} m).

> *Source*
>
> This graph comes from an article included in Boorse and Motz, *The world of the atom*, Volume II, page 1162. The article is 'Are electrons waves?' by Davisson, and should be very useful for teachers. It was originally published in the *Franklin Institute Journal* (1928), **205**, page 597.

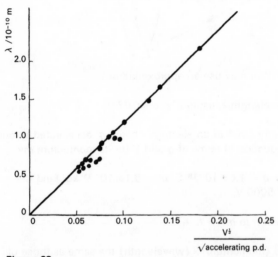

Figure 28
Wavelength of electrons against reciprocal of the square root of the accelerating voltage.
Based on Boorse, H. A., and Motz, L. (1966) The world of the atom, *Volume II, Basic Books.*

Momentum, not velocity, as the guide to wavelength

The experimental results show that the velocity of electrons is inversely proportional to wavelength. More evidence is needed to show that it is momentum, not just velocity, which decides the wavelength. To see what the evidence might be, we consider other particles, of different mass.

Q22 How much more slowly will a neutron have to travel than an electron if the two are to have the same momentum?

Such particles – neutrons and even gas molecules, which are of much greater mass than electrons – have been successfully diffracted, but to get momentum corresponding to a wavelength of 10^{-10} m, it is found that these heavier particles have to go very slowly – which makes the experiment hard to do. Neutron diffraction is now a tool used by physicists and others to supplement X-rays in the study of solids, as also is electron diffraction.

Matter waves are now out of the realm of speculation. We may not like, or understand them, but they are used every day as research tools. The relation $mv = h/\lambda$ says that for $\lambda \approx 10^{-10}$ m, $mv \approx 6 \times 10^{-24}$ kg m s^{-1}. A neutron has a mass of about 1.6×10^{-27} kg, so the kinetic energy at this momentum,

$$E = \frac{(mv)^2}{2m},$$

comes out close to 10^{-20} J, or less than 1/10 electronvolt. In a solid at room temperature, the molecules vibrate with energies of this size, and a good way to make neutrons suitable in wavelength for diffraction experiments is to let them pass into a warm solid and bounce about among the atoms.

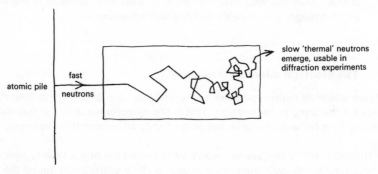

Figure 29
Slowing down of neutrons.

Soon they lose energy, by collision after collision, and end up in thermal equilibrium with the right energy for diffraction.

If not only electrons and neutrons, but all particles of matter have wave properties, is it feasible to think of ordinary lumps of matter (collections of particles), like a tennis ball, as having wave properties?

If one thought this, one could calculate the wavelength. It is then clear why the wave properties, if they exist, do not show up in experiments.

Q23 An electron, mass of order 10^{-30} kg, has a wavelength of 10^{-10} m at a velocity of order 10^7 m s^{-1}. Estimate the wavelength associated with a ball in a game of tennis.

Q24 What happens to a diffraction pattern as the wavelength is made smaller and smaller? What happens as the wavelength is made larger and larger? Why are X-rays and not visible light used to study crystal structures by diffraction methods? Why are diffraction effects with tennis balls never seen?

Film: 'Matter waves'

You should, if possible, see the film in which Davisson describes how he and Germer found electron diffraction. Some of their original apparatus is shown, and their experiments are repeated with modern improvements.

Film: 'Matter waves'

Guild Sound and Vision (see page 160).

This film makes an admirable summary here, but could be shown earlier or later. Students who saw the film at O-level may not need to see it again, though it is probably worth a second viewing.

The electron dilemma – reading

Which are electrons really – particles or waves? We have been here before: the answers are the same as for photons. This is the microscopic world of quanta. The inhabitants may behave strangely, but at least they all behave the same way.

Every student meeting this strange world for the first time needs time to become used to it; time to talk over the problems and to circle suspiciously round the ideas involved. As so many people have written so well about these problems, we suggest that you would do well to read some of the things they have said. As we pointed out at the beginning of this book, there are a number of reasons why this may be a worthwhile exercise, besides enabling you to become clearer about what the problem really is and how quantum behaviour is to be described.

Each reference that follows has a short commentary, telling you roughly what to expect. Following the references is a set of questions. You will do well to have the questions in mind as you read, and you may be asked to give answers to some of them.

Note to teachers

We suggest that each student should read one, at most two pieces, and that he should tell the others what answers he has found to the questions. Other tasks could be set: to write a short magazine article, or to write answers to a number of questions.

The Feynman passage is tough, but very worth while, as it gives a clear picture of how quanta behave. The chapters from PSSC and *Physics for the inquiring mind* are strongly recommended.

References

Feynman, *The Feynman lectures on physics,* Volume I, Chapter 37. This is difficult, but worth it. Concentrate on 37–1 to 37–5, without worrying about the algebra in 37–3. Feynman describes beautifully how the quantum world behaves, and you should read the words rather than the mathematics.

PSSC, *Physics*, 2nd edition, Chapter 33.
PSSC, *College physics*, Chapters 31, 33, 34. The chapter from the PSSC course gives information at about the right level for sixth form students. It is worth reading carefully. Section 33–7 is interesting because it compares the photon and the electromagnetic wave models of light. The three *College physics* chapters expand the same material.

Rogers, *Physics for the inquiring mind*, Chapter 44. This is a long chapter, and although you may like to read it all, the especially relevant parts are pages 723 (about photons) to 727, and pages 737 (particles and waves) to 742. The diagrams on pages 723, 725, 740, and 741 are very useful, as is the table at the top of page 738.

Born, *The restless Universe*, Chapter III. Max Born was one of the physicists who first explored the quantum world. He first suggested that chance or probability had to be used to describe the behaviour of particles. Pages 106–117 will be revision for most students. But read pages 117–121 about photons. You could skip pages 122–133 on spectra and Bohr's model of the atom; also skip pages 133–139 on the Compton effect and pages 139–151 which introduce electron waves. You should read pages 151–158 carefully. See especially plate III (b). The final pages, 159–165, are interesting, but could be missed.

Toulmin and Goodfield, *The architecture of matter*, Chapter 12. This is a fairly condensed historical account of the development of quantum ideas. Concentrate most on the section, 'Radiation is atomised'. You could stop at the point where Rutherford's nuclear model of the atom is discussed.

Project Physics, Reader, *Unit 5* contains a good chapter by Banesh Hoffmann.

Rothman, *The laws of physics*, Chapter 10. This is also historical, but less condensed than Toulmin and Goodfield. It is worth following up to page 180, but the final part ('The uncertainty principle') could be omitted. (Energy is measured on page 169 in ergs. 1 erg is equal to 10^{-7} joule.) If you have little time, omit pages 172–178 ('The size of a photon').

Caro, McDonell, and Spicer, *Modern physics*, Chapter 3. This chapter concerns the photo-electric effect, and the behaviour of photons. It is useful as a guide to which ideas come from experiment and which from theory.

Tolansky, *Revolution in optics*, Chapter 2. Do not bother with pages 33–37 on 'black body' radiation. Concentrate on pages 37 ('The photon') to 43. The remaining pages, 43–50, link up usefully with other parts of our work, but are less essential.

Bennet, *Electricity and modern physics*. Chapter 13.2–13.3 describes the photo-electric effect and the idea of photons rather briefly. There are several paragraphs describing the dual nature of light, and brief notes on spectra and the wave nature of particles.

Project Physics, Text, *Unit 5*. Chapter 18, section 18.4, discusses the photo-electric effect, and its interpretation is considered in 18.5. Section 18.6, on X-rays, is useful but less necessary. Chapter 20, sections 20.2 and 20.3, gives a good outline of the wave and particle behaviour of photons and electrons. (You will have to accept one formula from relativity.) Section 20.4 outlines the developments in quantum theory that will form most of the remaining work in our course.

Hoffmann, *The strange story of the quantum*. Chapter 8 discusses the ideas of de Broglie and the Davisson–Germer experiment. Electrons as waves and particles are discussed on pages 166–173. Chapter 3 discusses the photo-electric effect.

The Open University Science Foundation Course, Units 6 and 7, *Atoms, elements, and isotopes: atomic structure. The electronic structure of atoms.* See sections 6.4 and 6.5 on spectra and energy levels. Later Units dealing with quantum theory may also prove useful.

Now here are some questions to ask yourself as you read:

    a   Does the author say that $E = hf$ comes from experiment, from theory, from both, or from elsewhere?
    b   Does the author say that $mv = h/\lambda$ comes from experiment, theory, both, or neither? Are the answers for photons the same as for electrons, or not?
    c   Does the author say that the behaviour of electrons and photons can be deduced from deeper ideas?

d What does the author say about why the description of the quantum world is widely accepted?

e Does he say it is a final and true description? (Do you think he ought to?)

f Does he mention 'probability'? What does he say is probable or not probable?

g What is said to be random, unpredictable?

h What is said to be predictable?

i Does he explain why quantum effects are not seen on the large scale, for photons or for electrons?

j Does he say whether photons can vanish, unlike electrons? (Watch out for words like 'absorbed'.)

k Are photons said to have mass as well as momentum?

l Do you have the impression that in the development of these ideas, experiment led theory, theory led experiment, or a bit of both happened?

m Does he talk about 'models' or 'analogues' or 'pictures' (or some similar word) of photons or electrons?

n Does he say we have no adequate model of photons and electrons, or that we have two good models, or that we have a complicated model, or that we shouldn't expect to have a model? What do you think about these questions?

Waves of chance

What are these electron waves waves of? Nobody knows; most physicists have stopped trying to answer. The electron itself is the thing that is detectable, and that is no wave. The wave is a kind of ghost, telling how the electron is likely to travel. Just as for photons, the rule is: calculate the amplitude and square it to find the intensity, and that tells you how many electrons will arrive on average, or if you prefer, the chance that one electron will arrive.

To say that electrons interfere is just to say that they pile up one by one in the pattern in which a wave would arrive. It is not to say that electrons *are* waves, but that waves are needed to describe how electrons travel.

The only thing these waves have to do is to give an amplitude, such that

$$\text{chance of arrival} \propto (\text{amplitude})^2$$

can be calculated.

The rest of the paraphernalia of a wave model, that is, ups and downs, medium, push, pull, oscillations, are not used. No one has found a way to use them or give them meaning. The $(\text{amplitude})^2$ is all that counts. The rest is 'not there' at all, so far as observable events go, though the phase of the waves is an essential ingredient in adding up the total effect of several waves, whose total amplitude is then squared to find the intensity or probability.

The oldest rule in the book

' "It's the oldest rule in the book," said the King. . . .

It is a curious feature of the wave-and-particle description of light and of electrons that it uses old rules in new ways. The old physics of particles, using terms like momentum and energy, still has a place. The old physics of waves, with amplitudes being added together to calculate superposition effects, still has a place. The rules are the old rules, but their combination is new and startling. In combining them, physicists were forced to think very hard about the difference between events they could record, such as the arrival of energy carried by a photon, and things they could not, such as the oscillations of an electron wave, or which slit a photon passed through. And perhaps the need to remember the difference between what you can actually observe and measure, and what you cannot, really could be called the oldest rule in the book. The physics of quanta nevertheless gave physicists a sharp reminder of it.

Part Three

Waves in boxes

'"Is there any point to which you would wish to draw my attention?"
"To the curious incident of the dog in the night-time."
"The dog did nothing in the night-time."
"That was the curious incident," remarked Sherlock Holmes.'

A. Conan Doyle, The memoirs of Sherlock Holmes.

'That which changes in matter, the rusting blade, the hard coal turned smoke, is but a rearrangement of the same tiny particles. The chemist can recover the iron from rust, or the carbon from the hot gas, and the elements recovered differ in no whit from their counterparts in a sheltered sample. Atoms do not change!'

Professor Philip Morrison.

The stability of atoms

The idea that particles have wave properties turned out to be the key to understanding how it is that the atoms of an element are all so much alike, and stay alike, behaving in just the same way in chemical or physical experiments year after year. The Greeks first thought of atoms as a way of explaining how it is that matter can change, but still be recoverable: that water can freeze and then become water again, that iron can be obtained from the ore, rust away, and be recovered again. Their idea, since pursued by chemists, was that the changes in matter were to be thought of as changes in the *arrangement* of atoms, while the atoms themselves remained unchanged. This stability of atoms is an essential part of the explanation: matter is recognizable and behaves consistently; it is possible to do chemistry, just because atoms always behave in the same way.

For these reasons, atoms were for long thought of as hard, unchangeable spheres. which could not be broken into smaller pieces. But we now think that atoms do have parts: that they are electrons surrounding a nucleus, itself made of protons and neutrons. The electrons are often imagined revolving around the nucleus. This view gets us into several difficulties, as follows.

If such a 'solar system' atom hits another, the laws of dynamics say that the motion of the electrons in each must change, just as the Earth's orbit would change should another star pass close by. Yet the kinetic theory says that such collisions are happening all the time, at the rate of billions a second. How can a miniature solar system retain the same properties — size, spectrum, energy, and chemical properties — when subject to such a buffeting?

As with the dog in the night-time in the Sherlock Holmes story, the curious thing is that nothing happens.

New atoms can be minted (in nuclear reactors), yet they seem to behave exactly like all others of the same kind. But a 'solar system' atom could be put together in many ways, the 'planets' orbiting at any radius they please. Somehow, when the parts of an atom are put together, they choose the 'right' behaviour. There is evidence, seen earlier, that atoms exist with one of a limited number of energies; all atoms in, say, the lowest energy level being like all others in that level. But a 'solar system' atom is not confined to any particular energy by the ordinary laws of dynamics. Any energy should be possible. The very existence of energy levels demands a new kind of theory which goes beyond ordinary dynamics.

The 'solar system' model makes wrong predictions, too. Just as an electron oscillating in an aerial generates radio waves, so electromagnetic laws predict that electrons going round in orbit will radiate. (If we look at an orbit edge on, the electron will seem to be oscillating.) Such an orbiting electron will lose energy continually, spiralling inwards until it can go no further. But atoms do not radiate continually, and do tend to stay the same size. (Calculations show that if the orbiting electrons radiated energy, an atom would collapse in less than 10^{-10} s.)

Instead, as has been seen in Part One, atomic spectra can be explained by supposing that the atom jumps from energy level to energy level, radiating when it does so, but not radiating at all while in one particular level.

A new theory for atoms

These are some of the problems that led to a new kind of dynamics for atoms, called wave mechanics or quantum theory. A new theory must not just avoid the difficulties. It must (and can) explain why atoms behave as they do. For preference, it should also make new predictions, and that too was achieved. Here are some things that the theory can explain.

1 The size of atoms

For instance, a hydrogen atom is about 0.5×10^{-10} m in radius, as measured by various methods. Somehow, the electrical attraction of the proton for the electron fails to make the atom collapse any further.

Q1 Suggest some ways of measuring the size of atoms or ions. (Hints: X-rays; kinetic theory; thin films.)

2 The values of the energy levels

Hydrogen has levels at energies $21.8 \times 10^{-19}/n^2$ J below the energy at which the electron is torn free (the atom is ionized).

3 The existence of a lowest possible energy level

No hydrogen atom has ever been found with energy lower than 21.8×10^{-19} J below the energy for ionization.

We shall try to show something of how these things are explained. Quantum theory is more powerful than we can show in this course. It can help to explain the behaviour of nuclei as well as of atoms, though here there are many unsolved problems. It can explain how atoms that form molecules come to be bonded together, and why those that do not, do not. It can explain the chemists' Periodic Table, with its curious number patterns 2–8–8–18 and so on, of repeating properties. It can describe the rotations and vibrations of molecules that cause them to emit or absorb infra-red light. It has helped physicists to understand the strength of materials, and the electrical conductivity of metals. In fact, there are few sciences concerned with atoms and molecules that have been left untouched by the ideas of wave mechanics.

The arguments that follow
Reaching towards a theory of the hydrogen atom

The work of this part of the course now embarks upon a series of arguments in stages (stages one to three) which are intended to lead towards the final goal, an understanding of the quantum, or wave-particle theory of hydrogen atoms. The hydrogen atom is quite a complicated problem, and is as far as we shall go in detail. But the theory can be extended – with difficulty – to other atoms and molecules. and in Part Four we shall try to indicate finally the sort of results that can be obtained with more complicated problems. However, the hydrogen atom theory will mainly have to stand as a symbol for these other possible achievements.

Note for teachers
The Bohr theory

Bohr's theory of the hydrogen atom does not appear in any detail in this work. This is not because it is uninteresting or unimportant. Time is short, and although the Bohr theory is of great historical interest, it is misleading as a theory in that it is essentially not a wave theory at all. Nor are Bohr's orbits as real as they may seem: indeed in the ground state of hydrogen there is exactly zero orbital angular momentum, and the electron does not 'go round' the nucleus at all. There are plenty of good accounts of Bohr's theory (see below) and teachers may wish to fill in the historical background by describing it. Such a description should be regarded as additional to the work of this course.

Bohr theory: references

Boorse and Motz, *The world of the atom*, Volume II, page 734. (Biography and original paper.)

Born, *The restless Universe*, page 176.

Caro, McDonell, and Spicer, *Modern physics*, page 84.

Conn and Turner, *The evolution of the nuclear atom*, page 230. (Original paper.)

Rogers, *Physics for the inquiring mind*, page 731. (Good for student reading.)

Sherwin, *Basic concepts of physics*, page 228. (Out of print.)

Stage one
Order of magnitude arguments about hydrogen and about nuclei

At this stage, we shall see how to answer the following question: 'Why does the electrical pull of the proton on the electron not pull the electron in a hydrogen atom closer to the proton than a certain distance?'

The answer turns out also to explain why there cannot be electrons in the nucleus, why the gamma rays that emerge when neutrons combine with protons to make deuterons (heavy hydrogen) have high energy, and, in a general way, why solids are so very incompressible. We approach the first stage by thinking about waves which are confined to small space.

Q2 Electrons have wave properties. Electrons in an atom are kept close to the nucleus by electrical attraction. What kind of waves appear on a string or spring when the waves are kept inside a part of the string by fixing the ends?

Q3 What is the frequency of the lowest note obtainable on a guitar string of length 0.5 m, if waves travel on the string at 200 m s⁻¹?

Demonstration
10.8 Standing waves
a Standing waves on a stretched cord

When waves on a stretched cord are kept within two fixed ends, the cord does not vibrate at any frequency one may wish. Instead, if it is driven at varying frequencies, it responds only at definite frequencies. It does not respond at any frequency lower than that for the pattern of motion with one 'loop' shown at the top of figure 30. That is, a standing wave of wavelength longer than twice the length of the cord cannot be 'fitted in' at all.

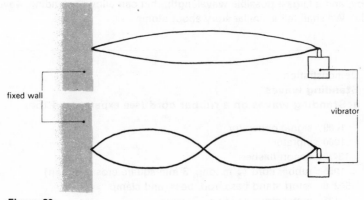

Figure 30

Perhaps an atom, in which the wave-like electrons are confined to a small space, may be thought of as being filled with standing waves.

b More complicated standing waves

An atom is a three-dimensional thing, not a long thin string. Look at standing waves on either a flat plate, a rubber diaphragm, or a springy ring. If there is time see more than one.

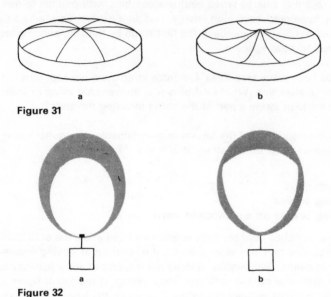

Figure 31

Figure 32

With these two-dimensional standing waves there is again a lowest possible frequency, and a largest possible wavelength, that can allow a standing wave to 'fit inside'. We shall tell a similar story about atoms.

Demonstration
10.8 Standing waves
a Standing waves on a rubber cord (see experiment 4.15c)

1009	signal generator
1060	vibrator
134/2	xenon flasher
1055	rubber cord ($\frac{1}{2}$ m long, 3 mm square cross-section)
503–6	retort stand base, rod, boss, and clamp
121	metal strips as jaws *2 pairs*
44/2	G-clamp (small) *2*
1000	leads

b **Vibrations in a rubber sheet** (see experiment 4.16e)

1009	signal generator
1044	large loudspeaker
134/2	xenon flasher
1053	sheet of rubber
503	retort stand base *2*
1076	large ring

Figure 33 *a* shows how the rubber cord may be stretched between jaws held in a clamp, and the vibrator, to which it may be tied. The cord should not be so taut as to prevent the vibrator from vibrating freely. White painted spots on a black rubber cord make for an effective demonstration, especially if the cord is viewed both in steady light and when illuminated by a stroboscope.

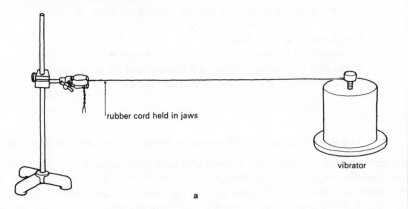

rubber cord held in jaws

vibrator

a

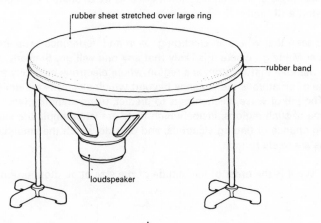

rubber sheet stretched over large ring

rubber band

loudspeaker

b

Figure 33
Standing wave experiments.

Figure 33 *b* shows how to excite oscillations in a rubber sheet. The sheet is stretched over the large metal ring, so as to be as evenly stretched as possible. Holding the sheet to the ring by a large rubber band makes it easy to make small adjustments of the evenness of the sheet's tension. The large loudspeaker is placed below the ring and rubber sheet. Frequencies in the range 10 to 100 Hz are required, and the larger the power delivered by the loudspeaker, the better. Try a central position of the speaker first, and a low frequency, and raise the frequency gradually, looking and listening for the lowest mode, in which the centre of the rubber sheet rises and falls. Radial lines drawn on the rubber make the oscillations easier to see. The amplitude may be 10 to 20 mm at the centre.

At a higher frequency, with the speaker off centre as in figure 30 *b*, a mode of oscillation can be found in which the rubber surface tilts, one side rising as the other falls, the rim staying fixed, of course.

Film loops (see page 160).
'Vibrations of a drum' shows the rubber diaphragm.
'Soap film oscillations' shows standing waves on soap films.
These two loops are not essential, but may be helpful.

The size of an atom: the region where electrons are likely to be

In work on ionic crystals (Unit 3, *Field and potential*), when Na^+ and Cl^- ions came within distances of less than about 3×10^{-10} m, large repulsive forces sprang up which held the ions in balance against their electrical attraction. It would be reasonable to think of the ions 'touching' at these distances, but all this means is that the electrons around an Na^+ ion started to try to share neighbouring space with those round a Cl^- ion.

We have seen that where an electron goes in an interference experiment is a matter of chance. Many go where it is likely that any one will go. Similarly, we shall develop the idea that an atom is a region where electrons are likely to be found. The edge of an atom is the distance beyond which electrons are unlikely to be found. The job of wave mechanics is to predict, using standing wave ideas, the size and shape of such regions, inside which there are large amplitude standing waves and a big chance of finding electrons, and outside which the amplitude is small and electrons are rarely found.

Q4 What is the order of magnitude of the size of an atom or ion?

A crude theory of hydrogen: waves in an atom-sized box

If electron waves are confined, as in an atom, to a space of size 10^{-10} m, certain important consequences follow, even from very rough guesses about the shape of the waves. The following questions explore these consequences for a hydrogen atom, composed of one proton and one electron.

Q5 In figure 34 a standing wave with one half wavelength 'loop' is shown fitting into a diameter of the space, so that $\lambda \approx 4 \times 10^{-10}$ m. Is this the largest or smallest possible wavelength that would fit across a diameter?

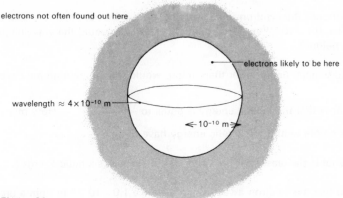

electrons not often found out here

electrons likely to be here

wavelength $\approx 4 \times 10^{-10}$ m

10^{-10} m

Figure 34

Q6 An electron of wavelength λ has momentum $mv = h/\lambda$. What value of momentum is associated with the above wavelength? ($h = 6.6 \times 10^{-34}$ J s.)

Q7 May the electron have less than this momentum, in the circumstances?

Q8 The electron has momentum mv at least equal to 1.6×10^{-24} kg m s^{-1}. What is the least possible kinetic energy $\dfrac{mv^2}{2}$? $m = 9.1 \times 10^{-31}$ kg. and

$$\frac{mv^2}{2} = \frac{(mv)^2}{2m}.$$

An electron confined within such a space must be moving around fairly rapidly, with kinetic energy at least 14×10^{-19} J, which is of the order of 10 electronvolts.

Q9 What prevents the electron with such kinetic energy from flying away from its proton?

Q10 What energy must be transferred to electrical potential energy for an electron to move from 1.0×10^{-10} m to a long distance from a proton (to become free)? ($e = 1.6 \times 10^{-19}$ C; $\dfrac{1}{4\pi\varepsilon_0} = 9 \times 10^9$ N m^2 C^{-2}.)

Q11   Has an electron with kinetic energy 14×10^{-19} J enough energy to escape from a distance of 1.0×10^{-10} m from a proton?

These arguments may be put the other way round. Electrical attraction between proton and electron is just capable of holding the electron within 1.0×10^{-10} m, because the short wavelength and large momentum demanded by this limit on size require a kinetic energy nearly equal to, but still less than, the electrical energy needed to tear the electron free.

But an atom cannot be much less than this size, as the following questions show.

Q12   Suppose the electron in a hydrogen atom were confined to a space ten times smaller, 0.1×10^{-10} m. How many times smaller would the wavelength have to be than before?

Q13   How many times larger than before would the momentum mv have to be?

Q14   Show that the kinetic energy is equal to $\dfrac{(\text{momentum})^2}{2m}$. How many times larger than before would the kinetic energy have to be?

Q15   What is the least possible value of the electron's kinetic energy?

Q16   To tear the electron away from a distance 1.0×10^{-10} m from a proton, energy 23×10^{-19} J had to be transferred to electrical potential energy. How much energy is needed if the distance is ten times smaller?

Q17   Would the electrical attraction be strong enough to keep the electron within a space 0.1×10^{-10} m across?

Summary of stage one
Why are atoms about 10^{-10} m in size

If the electron in a hydrogen atom were kept within a space much larger than 10^{-10} m across, the wavelength of the standing wave would be large and the momentum and so the kinetic energy would be small. The kinetic energy turns out to be less in magnitude than the electrical potential energy of the charged electron and proton. Thus the atom can 'afford' to be smaller, energy being transferred from electrical potential energy to kinetic energy. As the 'box' shrinks, the wavelength is reduced, and the momentum and kinetic energy rise as a result ($mv = h/\lambda$).

But the box cannot be made indefinitely smaller. There comes a point where the wavelength is so short that momentum implies the kinetic energy greater than the electrical energy binding the particles together. It is like squeezing down a box with a ball in it that rattles about faster and faster the smaller the box. If the box is made too small, the ball bursts through the walls. Figure 35 illustrates this idea.

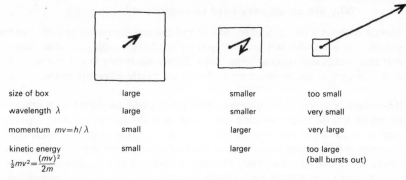

size of box	large	smaller	too small
wavelength λ	large	smaller	very small
momentum $mv = h/\lambda$	small	larger	very large
kinetic energy $\frac{1}{2}mv^2 = \frac{(mv)^2}{2m}$	small	larger	too large (ball bursts out)

Figure 35

Notice also that the energy predicted by the above calculations is about right. At 1.0×10^{-10} m radius, the electrical potential energy is -23×10^{-19} J, compared with the measured ionization energy of hydrogen -21.8×10^{-19} J (Part One).

The crude theory of hydrogen

A more formal version of essentially the same argument about the hydrogen atom as a box appears in Feynman, *The Feynman lectures on physics*, Volume I, Chapter 38.4. Teachers may like to look at it. By carefully choosing constants, the correct expressions for the Bohr radius and ionization energy come out. In the argument above, one could have chosen $\lambda = 2\pi r$ rather than $\lambda/2 = 2r$, when 'better' answers could have been extracted. But the constants would have been introduced *ad hoc*, and we prefer a rougher calculation. It is precisely when finding out how to fit waves correctly into a hydrogen atom that a fuller treatment, given later, comes into its own.

The rough calculation only shows that an electron can't be confined within 0.1×10^{-10} m, but could be confined within 1.0×10^{-10} m. To work out an equilibrium distance, it would be necessary to equate dV/dr for the electric potential to d (kinetic energy)$/dr$ — giving a calculation rather like that for ionic crystals in Unit 3, Part Four. This is not pursued because the argument is too rough to justify such detail. For example, the standing wave can't have a constant wavelength since V, and hence the electron's kinetic energy, must vary with r.

Why are solids very hard to compress?

Almost without it being noticed, one of the biggest puzzles in physics has been solved. It is a well-known fact that you do not fall through your chair (usually) or that steel struts will support large loads. Solids are strong in compression. Physics also tells us that the atoms in these things are nearly all empty space.

If two solar systems came together, they could easily penetrate each other. But atoms do not go on penetrating each other until the nuclei are close together: they stop at distances of the order of 10^{-10} m. This is because the electrical repulsion between the electrons tends to keep electrons away from the overlap region. As the atoms are forced together, each electron is confined to a smaller and smaller box, which means that it must have smaller wavelength, and so larger momentum and larger kinetic energy.

In Unit 3 a mysterious repulsion force had to be introduced to keep the ions of an ionic crystal in balance. The source of these repulsion forces that make solids hard to squash is now explicable. In squashing a solid we are trying to squeeze the electrons of each atom into a smaller space, and they will not do it. Or rather they will do it only if we supply the energy from outside. Calculations like those given above show that a small squeeze may require a lot of energy, which is why huge forces are needed to squash any solid.

Problems of the nucleus – electrons in the nucleus?

This discussion can throw some light on the problems of the nucleus, which is a very small box indeed, about 10^{-14} m across (Unit 5). It was once thought that a nucleus of mass A, charge $+Z$ might be made of A protons and $A - Z$ electrons, the electrons being held to the protons by electrical forces. Similarly, people have thought of a neutron as a proton plus an electron, held together electrically. Both views must be wrong. Why? Because in a box of size 10^{-14} m, $\lambda \approx 10^{-14}$ m, mv comes to 10^{-19} kg m s^{-1}. The kinetic energy is $(mv)^2/2m$, which is 10^{-9} J for electrons, that is, 10^{10} electronvolts. There are no known forces which could hold down electrons with so large a kinetic energy: the electrical energy of attraction at 10^{-14} m is only 10^5 electronvolts or 10^{-14} J (as may be calculated knowing its order of magnitude at 10^{-10} m, from question 10 above).

Electrons cannot be squeezed down within nuclear sizes by electrical forces. Can protons? We explore this next.

The energy of particles within the nucleus

Not much is understood about the forces which hold nuclei together, but at least they must be strong enough to contain protons or neutrons within regions of size about 10^{-14} m across. The particles must have wavelength λ of this order of magnitude or less. As before:

The size determines the largest wavelength λ.

Momentum $mv = \dfrac{h}{\lambda}$ at least.

Kinetic energy $= \dfrac{(mv)^2}{2m} = \dfrac{h^2}{2m\lambda^2}$ at least.

Q18 Find the least kinetic energy of a neutron or proton contained within a space such that $\lambda = 10^{-14}$ m or less. Look up values of h and m.

Q19 Convert the energy in question 18 to electronvolts ($e = 1.6 \times 10^{-19}$ C).

The above calculation suggests that the kinetic energy of particles within a nucleus will be of the order of 10 MeV. The energy with which nuclear forces bind them together must be at least as large as this; it turns out not to be very much larger, in fact. To take a case where the evidence is fairly simple, we consider the nucleus made of one proton and one neutron, the deuteron.

When neutrons from a reactor are fired at protons (in water or wax, for example), the protons may capture neutrons in a way not unlike the capture of electrons by protons to make hydrogen atoms. In the latter process, light is emitted at many frequencies, up to the limit where the photon energy is equal to 21.8×10^{-19} J, the difference in energy between a free electron and one in the lowest energy level of hydrogen (see Part One). When protons capture neutrons, to form deuterons, 'light' is emitted in the form of gamma rays of just one energy, 2.2 MeV.

Q20 How many energy levels has a deuteron?

If wave ideas are used to calculate other possible wave states for a deuteron, they show that all the states one can imagine have kinetic energies greater than the energy with which the deuteron is bound together. Thus only one state exists, that with energy 2.2 MeV below 'freedom', for which the kinetic energy comes out to be 2.2 MeV less than the potential energy with which the deuteron is bound.

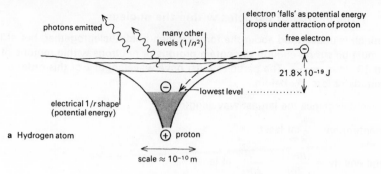

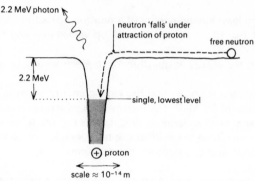

b Deuteron nucleus

Figure 36

Reading

PSSC *College physics*, Chapter 35, gives a good account of atomic, molecular, and nuclear binding, and could be used to bring together the theoretical arguments and experimental evidence presented so far.

A photograph of the deuteron formation gamma ray spectrum appears on page 664, while pages 666–667 show how the many nuclear energy levels of a complex nucleus may be mapped out, using methods very like those employed for atomic energy levels in electron bombardment techniques (Unit 2, Part Five).

Other nuclei have many energy levels, typically with energies of a few million electronvolts, spaced at intervals of the order 0.1 million electronvolts. The levels can be investigated experimentally by firing particles of known energy at nuclei, and seeing how much energy they give up. This method is exactly analogous to the method discussed in Unit 2, Part Five, for finding the energy levels of atoms by firing electrons at them. Theoretical work is still going on to see if the levels of various nuclei can be explained theoretically. Too little is known about nuclear forces for any but partial successes to have been achieved so far. Ultimately, theorists would like to be able to explain the existence of the many sub-atomic particles themselves as different energy states of a smaller set of objects. This is no more than a dream at present.

A possible place to stop

This is a place to ask students if they want to go further. The achievements are limited, but the character of the arguments has been exposed, and it might be sensible to stop here, and pass to a brief version of Part Four. With many classes, it would be best to do so, and would certainly be better than wearying them with ideas in which they cannot sustain an interest.

We hope that some students, and some classes, will want to explore the ideas a little further. Stage two will be enough for most, while a few may continue through stage three. Both stages show how the ideas can be used to make more detailed and more accurate predictions. As it is the range and quality of its predictions that make quantum theory a great theory, we hope some will pursue the ideas as far as they can. If it can be arranged, it would be good if those students who wanted to could go on, while others were employed on other matters. But no student should feel ashamed of stopping here (with a brief look at Part Four): he or she has seen already the main dilemmas of quantum physics, and the sort of way they are resolved.

Teachers who pass here to Part Four should look particularly at examples 4, 'The number patterns 2–8–8–18, and so on, in the Periodic Table', 6, 'How a molecule is held together', and 7, 'The water molecule'.

Stage two
Electron standing waves in a 1/*r* shaped 'box'

Note to teachers

In this stage, we show how the shape of the 'box' in which electron standing waves are trapped affects the allowed wavelengths, and so decides the allowed energies, or energy levels. We shall give an argument for the $1/n^2$ rule of the energy levels of hydrogen atoms. In stage three, a numerical solution of a one-dimensional Schrödinger equation will be shown. That argument will require students to understand how the potential energy varying as $1/r$ determines the kinetic energy, and so the effective wavelength at any distance *r*. These ideas are developed and used in stage two.

However, the results of stage two are substantial enough for it to be possible to stop there, omitting stage three. It will still be possible to follow as much of Part Four as students wish.

Towards a better version of the theory

The crude wave-particle argument used so far has given a taste of the ideas behind the new wave mechanics. But the real job of the theory is to do what has so far been neglected: to say just how the waves do fit into atoms or nuclei, and so to obtain more information about their behaviour. For the hydrogen atom, for example, how does a wave-electron behave in an inverse square force? What waves are allowed? That is the kind of question we have to ask.

In stage one, we thought of an atom, or a nucleus, as being like a box in which electrons and their waves are trapped. In stage two, we shall be more realistic, and as a result, make the theory yield information about the $1/n^2$ rule for the energy levels of the hydrogen atom and the size of the atom. That this process of improving a theory is possible may be a valuable lesson in itself. It often happens in science that one has to feed into a theory more or less inadequate assumptions. It is often the case that the better the assumptions the more detailed and reliable are the predictions, but that the mathematics becomes harder to do. A scientist has to learn to choose just the right level of adequacy of assumptions for the kind of answer he needs.

The hydrogen atom – an electrical 'box'

An electron trapped in a box is not unlike a person locked in a room. An electron in a hydrogen atom is not much like either of these.

Q21 Suppose you are blindfolded and locked in an empty room. You take a few steps. How is your motion changed if you **a** do, **b** do not reach a wall? When will you feel strong forces?

Q22 Now suppose you are blindfolded, and in a field in which another person is standing, holding a prize. He blows occasional sharp bursts on a whistle, and you move towards the whistle when you hear it. The louder you hear it, the quicker you move. Why is this situation rather more like that of an electron held near a proton than is the situation of question 21?

In stage one, we calculated the kinetic energy of a trapped electron by finding first the momentum mv, from the wavelength λ of a standing wave, using de Broglie's relation

$$mv = \frac{h}{\lambda}.$$

Then the kinetic energy $\frac{1}{2}mv^2$ could be calculated.

Because it is easy to link the *energy* of the electron with the wavelength of a standing wave, it is best to describe not the forces, but the changes in *energy* produced by the electrical attractions between proton and electron in a hydrogen atom.

Q23 Figure 37 shows two kinds of elephant trap. Which is more like the electron-trap set by a proton? Which is more like the model used in stage one?

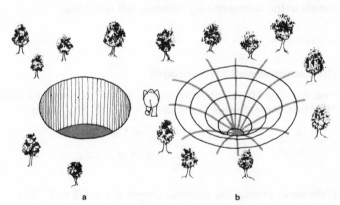

Figure 37　　　　　　　a　　　　　　　　　　　b

Physicists call such an electron-trap a 'potential well'. A hole, or a well (like figure 37 *a*) is a place where the gravitational potential energy of an object that has fallen into it is less than that of one which is 'free'. To become free, a trapped object must acquire potential energy. In the electric field of a proton, an electron which moves closer to the proton, or 'falls', then has less potential energy than before. To get a long way from the proton – to become free – the electron must acquire potential energy.

It is convenient, and conventional, to call the potential energy of a free, untrapped electron zero. If this is done, its potential energy when in the trap will have to be less than zero, that is, be given a negative value. This means only that the electron must acquire energy in order to 'climb' out. This convention was referred to in Part One.

Potential wells – a good but slightly dangerous metaphor

Physicists often use metaphors, but need to remember that, like all metaphors, each has its limits. A radio telescope is said to 'see' a source; an electron is said to 'feel' a force. Neither description is meant literally. A 'well' is just such another metaphor, vivid but not in exact correspondence to the situation it illuminates.

A ball rolling inside a hollowed-out space is not exactly analogous to a ball which moves in a straight line and is restrained by forces acting along that line. The first ball rises up the sides of the well, the sides producing a horizontal component of change of velocity. The second ball does not move vertically at all. If the interchange of kinetic and potential energies of the two balls follows the same relationship with position, the two problems are in some way analogous. Thus, in Unit 5, a hill shaped to a $1/r$ curve was used as an analogy for the motion of an alpha particle in a potential varying as $1/r$. Nevertheless, the analogy is not a complete one, and a ball moving on a real hill or in a real bowl will make motions that a particle in the corresponding potential will not make.

The potential well for hydrogen

In Part Three, question 10, the potential energy V of an electron at a distance of 1.0×10^{-10} m from a proton was found to be -23×10^{-19} J, using

$$V = \frac{q_1 q_2}{4\pi\varepsilon_0 r} \qquad \begin{aligned} q_1 &= q_2 = 1.6 \times 10^{-19} \text{ C.} \\ \frac{1}{4\pi\varepsilon_0} &= 9 \times 10^9 \text{ N m}^2 \text{ C}^{-2}. \end{aligned}$$

Q24 Write down at once the potential energy at $r = 0.5 \times 10^{-10}$ m.

Table 7 gives values of the (negative) electrical potential energy V of an electron and a proton at distances from $r = 2.0 \times 10^{-10}$ m to $r = 0.1 \times 10^{-10}$ m.

$r/10^{-10}$ m	0.1	0.2	0.3	0.4	0.5	0.6	0.7	0.8	0.9	1.0
$V/10^{-19}$ J	230	115	77	57.5	46	38.4	33	28.9	25.5	23

$r/10^{-10}$ m	1.2	1.4	1.6	1.8	2.0
$V/10^{-19}$ J	19.1	16.4	14.4	12.8	11.5

Table 7
Potential energy of an electron at various distances from a proton.

Plot V against r, as in figure 38, using similar scales. It is best to leave a space above the r axis for later use (see figures 56 and 59).

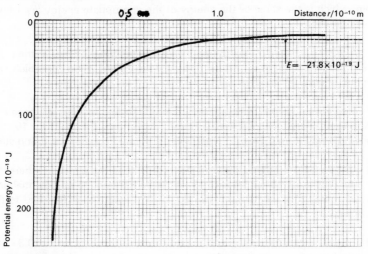

Figure 38
Variation of potential energy with distance for an electron near a proton.

Later use of 1/r graph (figure 38)

The graph carries the numerical values of the hydrogen potential well in accessible form. It will first be used in arguments in this stage. In stage three, the space above the r axis can be used for drawing one graphical solution of the Schrödinger equation – the standing wave equation for an atom.

Q25 This potential well or electron trap is a bottomless well. Why doesn't the electron fall down and down and down . . .? (*Hard* but look at stage one again.)

Finding the kinetic energy of the electron

We shall use the graph of the potential well (figure 38) to find the kinetic energy of the electron at various distances r from the proton. We do this because, given the kinetic energy, we can compute the momentum and so also the wavelength. Given the wavelength, which turns out to vary from place to place, we shall try to fit standing waves inside the potential well.

A hydrogen atom in its lowest energy level has to acquire an energy of 21.8×10^{-19} J for the electron to escape and become free. Draw a horizontal line across your copy of the potential well graph at energy $E = -21.8 \times 10^{-19}$ J, as shown in figure 38. We shall write E to mean the net energy of the electron in the atom, which is the same as the energy of the appropriate energy level (see table 4, page 26).

Q26 A 10^3 kg car freewheeling uphill acquires potential energy at the rate of about 10^4 joules per metre of vertical rise. At what height will a car which started with kinetic energy 10^5 J stop?

Q27 Use your potential well graph (figure 38) to find at what distance r according to ordinary mechanics, an electron with energy $E = -21.8 \times 10^{-19}$ J will stop moving away from a proton. What will be its kinetic energy at that distance?

Q28 If the electron moves closer to the proton than the distance where its kinetic energy is zero (about 1.1×10^{-10} m) what happens to its potential energy V? If the total energy E is constant, at -21.8×10^{-19} J, what then happens to the kinetic energy?

Q29 Use the potential well graph to find the kinetic energy at $r = 0.3 \times 10^{-10}$ m, if the total energy $E = -21.8 \times 10^{-19}$ J.

Rule for finding the kinetic energy

The total energy E is constant. Close to the proton, at small radii, the potential energy falls and the kinetic energy rises. If at radius r the potential energy is V, the kinetic energy is $(E-V)$. This can be read off the graph as the distance shown as $\updownarrow$ on figure 39. We shall use this rule repeatedly, because the kinetic energy decides the wavelength.

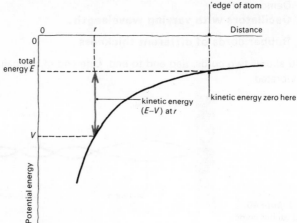

Figure 39
Finding the kinetic energy at distance r.

Standing waves with variable wavelength

We have now found that the kinetic energy of the electron near to the proton is larger than the kinetic energy further away, if the total energy remains constant. The momentum will change in a similar way. In working these ideas out, we have been treating the electron as a particle. Now we shall try to treat it as a wave instead, but at the same time try to make the wave obey the same rules as the particle would have to. The key to this is the expression for the wavelength:

$$\lambda = h/mv.$$

If the wave is to behave like the particle, then the wavelength λ might be small close to the proton where the momentum is large, and may increase further away as the momentum falls.

Ordinary dynamics tells us that the electron cannot be further away from the proton than the distance at which $E = V$ and the kinetic energy is zero (question 28). Presumably the wave dies away to zero somewhere near that distance. But can standing waves of variable wavelength occur? All the waves on strings and springs seen so far have had one fixed wavelength. The following demonstrations show that variable wavelength standing waves are perfectly possible.

Demonstration
10.9 Oscillators with varying wavelength

a Rubber cords of different thickness

Figure 40 shows two cords, tied end to end. One end of the pair is fixed, and the other is vibrated.

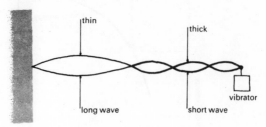

Figure 40
Oscillating rubber cords.

Q30 Do both cords vibrate with the same frequency?

Q31 On which cord do the waves travel more slowly? (Use what you know about the speed of waves on cords from Unit 4.)

Q32 Why have the standing waves on the thick cord the shorter wavelength?

b A hanging chain

A hanging chain (figure 41) carries more load at the top than at the bottom. Waves on a tight rope travel faster than on a slack rope. By shaking the top, standing waves can be made whose wavelength is smaller at the bottom than at the top, because the velocity is smaller at the bottom than at the top.

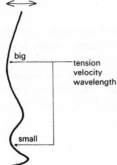

Figure 41
Oscillating hanging chain.

c Rubber strip of varying width

This is perhaps the prettiest. A V-shaped length of rubber is vibrated at the narrow end (figure 42).

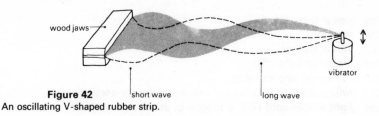

Figure 42
An oscillating V-shaped rubber strip.

Where waves travel slowly, on the more massive wide part, the wavelength is short. It increases slowly along the strip, being long at the narrow end where waves travel fast.

It is worth looking at the lowest frequency of vibration: the standing wave with one loop (figure 43).

Figure 43
Lowest mode of V-shaped rubber strip.

The peak is not in the middle, but near the wide end. Near that end, the rubber curves more sharply than at the other, just as it would have to do if there were many short waves at that end and few longer ones at the other. The wave in a hydrogen atom will look very similar, and we shall need to describe how 'curved' it is in terms of long or short .wavelengths.

In every case, the velocity varies from place to place. The frequency is the same at all places, so the wavelength must vary from place to place. These are standing waves in which a wavelength, adjusted to the proper value for each place, must fit into a finite region.

Demonstration
10.9 Oscillators with varying wavelength

    1009   signal generator
    1060   vibrator
    134/2 xenon flasher
    1055   length of light chain
    1055   V-shaped strip of rubber
    1055   rubber cord (0.5 m long, 3 mm square cross-section)
    1055   light rubber cord (0.5 m long; e.g. dressmaking elastic)

a Rubber cords of different thickness

See figure 40. Tie the thick rubber cord to the thin elastic, and fix one to the vibrator. Since the wave velocity depends on the square root of the mass per unit length, an effective demonstration requires cords having a mass ratio of at least four. Good lighting is important.

b Hanging chain

See figure 41. The sort of chain sold for securing bath plugs is suitable. It is easiest to swing the top round in a small circle, but it will be clearer ·that a standing wave is involved if the top is oscillated sideways.

c Rubber strip of varying width

See figures 42 and 43. Rubber cot sheet is a suitable material, cut with a razor blade along previously marked lines, while being held down and lightly stretched. A piece 0.5 m long, tapering from 100 mm to 10 mm, is about right. A line drawn down the middle helps to make the motion clear, especially as the edges of the strip tend to flap. Stroboscopic illumination along the length of the strip is very effective. Use as large an amplitude of oscillation as can be managed.

Standing waves in spherical atoms – a piece of geometry

The standing waves shown in demonstration 10.9 were all waves on a straight line, or one-dimensional standing waves, though 10.8 showed two-dimensional standing waves. But an atom is a three-dimensional object. One might perhaps hope that some at least of its electron standing waves would have the waves (and so also the chance of finding an electron) spread out uniformly round the nucleus in all directions. To put it more shortly – the atom may be a sphere, at least sometimes. Luckily, there is a mathematical theorem which relates one-dimensional standing waves along a line to spherically symmetrical standing waves.

Recall that the square of the amplitude of the electron standing wave is proportional to the chance of finding an electron. In a wave on a straight line, if the amplitude is A at some place, the chance of finding an electron *near that place* is proportional to A^2. The theorem says that we can treat spherical standing waves in a simple way. Pretend there is a one-dimensional standing wave from the centre out along one radius, and find the amplitude A at any radius r. Then $A^2\,dr$ represents the chance of finding an electron *near that radius* in any direction; that is, in the wall thickness dr of a spherical shell of radius r around the centre (figure 44).

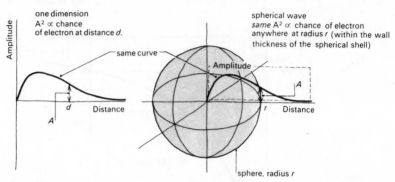

Figure 44

Spherical symmetry

The above passage, on spherically symmetrical waves, represents the largest piece of evasion in this work. No simple reasoning can be offered in its favour, but the result has no physical content. It is a happy accident of three dimensions. The less it is emphasized the better.

In one dimension, a standing wave ψ can be represented by

$$\frac{d^2\psi}{dx^2} = -k^2\psi.$$

In three dimensions, this becomes:

$$\frac{\partial^2\psi}{\partial x^2}+\frac{\partial^2\psi}{\partial y^2}+\frac{\partial^2\psi}{\partial z^2} = -k^2\psi.$$

Transforming to polar co-ordinates, if there is no variation with angle (spherical symmetry) geometry transforms the above into

$$\frac{1}{r}\frac{\partial^2(r\psi)}{\partial r^2} = -k^2\psi \qquad or$$

$$\frac{\partial^2 A}{\partial r^2} = -k^2 A.$$

Now $A^2 = r^2\psi^2$, and $\psi^2 dv$ represents the chance of having an electron in a small volume dv at one place, $r^2\psi^2 dr$ represents (apart from a constant 4π) the chance of having the electron in the volume $4\pi r^2 dr$, that is, at all points in a shell between radii r and $r+dr$. A^2 will be zero when $r = 0$.

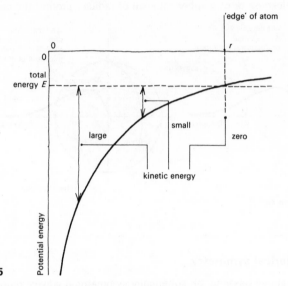

Figure 45

Fitting standing waves into a hydrogen atom

Figure 45 recalls the discussion of the kinetic energy of an electron of total energy E near to a proton, page 80. Close to the proton, the kinetic energy and momentum are large, the wavelength small. At larger radius r, the kinetic energy and momentum are less, the wavelength more, using $\lambda = h/mv$. The 'edge' of the atom is the radius at which $E = V$, where the kinetic energy is zero.

Q33 Parts a–d in figure 46 show some possible waves of varying wavelength 'fitted into' the space between $r = 0$ and the 'edge' of the atom. Which of the waves shown in a–d have the right kind of variation of wavelength with radius? (Recall demonstration 10.9.)

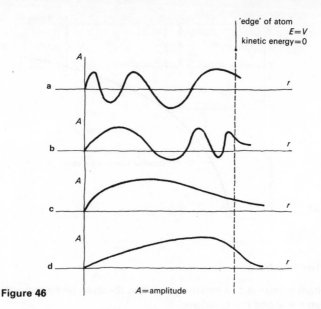

Figure 46
A=amplitude

All the waves start with zero amplitude at $r = 0$, because each might represent the chance of finding electrons within the wall thickness of a spherical shell of radius r. The volume of the shell wall shrinks to zero at $r = 0$. Electrons are not often found at very small radii because there is so little room for them. The chance per unit volume may be quite high (it is, in fact) but the volume itself is small.

Estimation of average wavelength for the lowest level of hydrogen

One way of fitting in a wave of varying wavelength would be to find an average wavelength. To find the average wavelength, an average value of the kinetic energy is needed. We shall make such a calculation for the lowest level of a hydrogen atom, whose energy $E = -21.8 \times 10^{-19}$ J.

As the kinetic energy is zero at radius r, where $E = V$, the value at radius $r/2$ might do as an average. This kinetic energy 'half way out' will be equal to E, as shown in figure 47, because the potential V follows a $1/r$ law, doubling as r is halved. We shall take the value E as a rough average value for the varying kinetic energy.

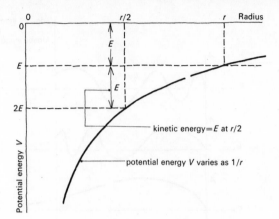

Figure 47

Note for teachers

If the total energy is E, a negative quantity, the average kinetic energy between $r = 0$ and $r = r_0$, where

$$E = \frac{e^2}{4\pi\varepsilon_0 r_0}$$

is given by:

average kinetic energy $= \displaystyle\int_0^{r_0}\left(E + \frac{e^2}{4\pi\varepsilon_0 r}\right)r^2\,\mathrm{d}r \Big/ \int_0^{r_0} r^2\,\mathrm{d}r$

if we assume the electron to be uniformly distributed in a sphere of radius r_0.

Therefore average kinetic energy $= E + \dfrac{3}{2}\dfrac{e^2}{4\pi\varepsilon_0 r_0}$.

Therefore average kinetic energy $= \frac{1}{2}\left|E\right|$.

See the article by Professor Mott in *Sources of physics teaching*, volume I, for a similar argument.

In the estimation above, we have set the average kinetic energy equal to E, not $\frac{1}{2}E$. Note also that the very large kinetic energies near $r = 0$ do not contribute much, for the electron is rarely there.

Q34 Take E as approximately 20×10^{-19} J and estimate the mean momentum of the electron. ($m = 9.1 \times 10^{-31}$ kg, or 10^{-30} kg. Momentum $= \sqrt{2m}$ (kinetic energy), since momentum $= mv$ and kinetic energy $= \frac{1}{2}mv^2$.

Q35 What is the mean wavelength? ($\lambda = h/mv$; $h = 6.6 \times 10^{-34}$ J s.)

The mean wavelength comes to about 3×10^{-10} m. Half a wavelength is about 1.5×10^{-10} m. But the wave has to fit into a space between $r = 0$ and roughly $r = 1.0 \times 10^{-10}$ m. It is clear that no more than one half wavelength can fit in. (The discrepancy between 1.5×10^{-10} m and 1.0×10^{-10} m is a result of the roughness of the approximation. We shall do better later on. It rather suggests that the wave might go beyond the 'edge' of the atom, and that turns out to be quite true.)

Figure 48 shows what the wave might be like. Compare figure 46 c.

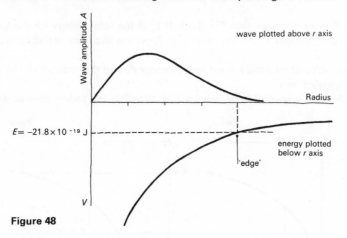

Figure 48

A success of the wave-particle theory

The wave sketched in figure 48 is the standing wave imagined for the *lowest* energy level of hydrogen. It turns out to have only one loop, which is the *least possible number of loops* in a standing wave. Recall that the lowest member of any standing wave family has just one loop half a wavelength long. In stage one, page 65, we *assumed* that the lowest energy level must have a one-loop wave. Now we see that it *does*. The measured energy E of the lowest energy level does correspond to a wavelength which gives the lowest member of a standing wave family. The theory can explain why there is a lowest possible energy level, and why it occurs with an energy of about -20×10^{-19} J.

In introducing Part Three, it was pointed out that any model of an atom involving electrons moving round a nucleus would make it difficult to explain why atoms are so alike and so stable, if ordinary dynamics applies. But this new theory which links momentum to wavelength can deal with the problem. The atom cannot collapse further because there are no possible lower standing wave patterns. Atoms in the lowest level are alike because there is just one standing wave pattern, so just one possible energy.

More theoretical explanation – the $1/n^2$ rule for energy levels of hydrogen

The theory, even in the rough 'average wavelength' version we are using at the moment, can explain why there are a series of energy levels, and the origin of the $1/n^2$ rule for their energies discovered by Balmer (page 28). Questions 36–41 show how.

Q36 The lowest energy level, index number $n = 1$, has a standing wave with $n = 1$ loop. How will a wave theory explain the existence of other energy levels?

Q37 The Balmer rule says that $E \propto 1/n^2$. If E_1 is the total energy for the level $n = 1$, what is the energy E_2 for the level $n = 2$, with a two-loop standing wave?

Q38 Figure 49 *a* shows the lowest level, energy E, and the radius r of the 'edge of the atom, where $E = V$.
Figure 49 *b* shows the second level, energy $E/4$. Why has the radius risen to $4r$?

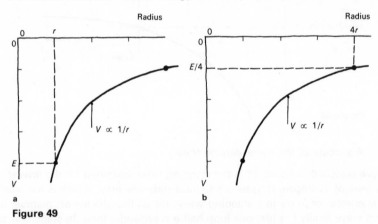

Figure 49

Q39 The standing wave for the level $n = 2$ now has two loops, to be fitted into four times the radius, as suggested in figure 50 *a* and *b*. Why has the mean wavelength doubled?

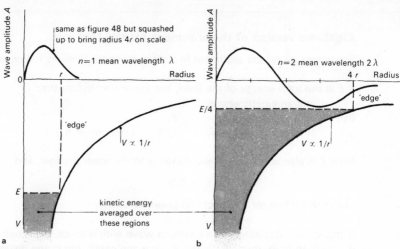

Figure 50

The new energy $E/4$ means a new mean kinetic energy. In figure 50 *b* with energy $E/4$, the kinetic energy averaged over the shaded region out to radius $4r$ includes more small values than in the shaded region in figure 50 *a*. The mean kinetic energy must have fallen, just as the energy E has fallen. The new mean kinetic energy means there is a new mean momentum and wavelength. *If, and only if*, the new mean wavelength turns out to have just doubled, will a wave, as shown in figure 50 *b*, just fit into the new space required. The next two questions show that it actually does fit.

Q40 Earlier arguments (question 34) gave:

1 Momentum $= \sqrt{2m \text{ (kinetic energy)}}$ since momentum $= mv$ and kinetic energy $= \frac{1}{2}mv^2$.

2 Mean kinetic energy may be equal to E approximately. Supposing only that the mean kinetic energy is proportional to the total energy E then:

mean momentum $\propto \sqrt{E}$ using **1**.

In going from the level $n = 1$ to the level $n = 2$, the $1/n^2$ rule reduces E to $E/4$. What happens to the mean momentum?

Q41 $\lambda = h/mv$. What has happened to the mean wavelength?

The new energy $E/4$ is just right. Question 39 shows that, for $n = 2$, this new energy leads to a bigger atom which would need a wave of doubled wavelength to fit into it. Question 41 shows that the wavelength obtained with energy $E/4$ is in fact just doubled, so the wave does just fit in as question 39 requires it to do. The Balmer $1/n^2$ rule is the result of making the waves fit into an electrical box with a $1/r$ shape. The whole numbers n appear because atoms are standing wave systems and a standing wave may only have a whole number of loops.

Algebraic version of the argument for the $1/n^2$ rule

Some may prefer the argument in a more compact form, as follows.

If E is the total energy of the level, we assume as before that:

mean kinetic energy $\propto E$.

But   mean momentum $\propto \sqrt{E}$.

So   mean wavelength $\lambda \propto 1/\sqrt{E}$ since $mv = h/\lambda$.

Now E is also related to r_0, the distance to the atom's 'edge', and

$$r_0 \propto 1/E$$

from the $1/r$ law for the electrical potential energy.

If the atom is described by a standing wave with n loops, each half a wavelength long, then, if λ is the mean wavelength and r_0 the distance, the waves must fit into the box with n loops in distance r:

$$n\lambda \propto r_0.$$

Thus $$n\left(\frac{1}{\sqrt{E}}\right) \propto \left(\frac{1}{E}\right)$$

using the dependence of λ and r_0 on E.

Simplifying this gives

$$n\sqrt{E} = \text{constant}$$

or $$E \propto \frac{1}{n^2}, \text{ which is the Balmer rule.}$$

Quantum theory's description of atoms

So far, we have only made rough sketches of the shapes of possible standing waves, and have done some order of magnitude calculations. It is possible, but harder, to compute the actual shape of the standing waves for simple atoms. You may like to look at figures 60 to 65 (pages 108 to 111) which show accurately calculated wave shapes for some energy levels of hydrogen. How they were calculated is explained in stage three, and one of them is worked out.
But even without further detailed calculation, you have already seen the essence of the ideas.

As we promised at the start of stage two, it has been possible to improve the theory so that it will explain a good deal about a hydrogen atom. The atom's size and the energies it can have can be found by discovering the standing waves that will fit into it. Their amplitude at a place predicts the chance that an electron will occupy the region near that place.

The two-humped wave for $n = 2$ (figure 50 b) shows that an electron, for a hydrogen atom with the 'right' energy, will often be at one of two distances from the proton. The accurate picture, figure 63, shows that it will more often be at the larger distance, which has the bigger hump. As the electron may be anywhere around the proton, this wave predicts that the electron will usually inhabit a pair of fuzzy regions around the proton. For $n = 3$, there are three such regions. See figure 70, page 121.

These shells are some of the 'orbitals' of which chemists often speak. They are the humps of standing waves: waves the square of whose amplitude predicts the chance that an electron will be within a fixed region of space.

Pythagoras explained the music of the lyre in terms of whole numbers, which we now describe in terms of wave-loops on its strings. Quantum theory explains the music of atomic spectra in a similar way, in terms of whole numbers of wave-loops fitting into atoms.

The makers of quantum theory

Quantum theory was the work of many people, notably Schrödinger, Heisenberg, and Born. Schrödinger, building on de Broglie's wave-particle ideas, was responsible for introducing the wave idea into the theory of atoms. The theory was developed over the years 1924 to 1930, but it grew out of an important earlier theory.

This earlier theory was the work of Bohr, who thought of it soon after Rutherford had produced his model of atoms containing small nuclei surrounded by electrons. Bohr's theory was a somewhat makeshift affair, but was nevertheless of the first importance.

Bohr's theory was an orbit theory of hydrogen. The electrons were supposed to keep to certain definite orbits, each with a definite energy, and never to travel in other orbits in between.

Waves were not mentioned in the theory. It had two big weaknesses. Firstly, it went wrong for atoms heavier than hydrogen. Secondly, and this was a more serious fault, it could not say why some orbits were allowed and others not although it told you how to calculate which ones were allowed.

The importance of the theory was that it worked, however shakily. The ingredients: h, m, e, and the electric potential of a charge, were used to calculate the energy of hydrogen atoms for the first time. Bohr brilliantly produced the formula for the energy of any level:

$$E_n = \frac{1}{n^2}\left(\frac{2\pi^2 m}{h^2}\right)\left(\frac{e^2}{4\pi\varepsilon_0}\right)^2$$

How he got it is no longer of such interest: the important thing was that he made people realize that you could put together the mass and charge of an electron, ε_0, and Planck's constant, and explain the hydrogen levels. From that time the search for a better theory increased in intensity. It took many years, and was achieved by the combined efforts of de Broglie (the wave idea), Heisenberg, Born (the idea of waves deciding chance), Schrödinger (an equation for the waves), and later Dirac who gave the theory even deeper foundations, showing that the wave idea was just one possible way of looking at the problem.

The new theory has come to be called wave mechanics or quantum mechanics.

End of stage two: another place to stop

This completes stage two, and many classes will wish to stop Part Three, 'Waves in boxes', here and go on to look at material from Part Four which illustrates in principle how quantum theory can be developed further and how powerful it is.

Stage three has something to offer the more mathematically inclined. The crudities of averaging the wavelength are abandoned, and the way in which accurate solutions can be found is illustrated. Earlier work with graphical solutions finds a new and exciting use.

Stage three uses a computer-made film, which shows solutions being calculated and displayed graphically. Figures 60 to 65 are a set of frames from such a film. Students who omit stage three might still enjoy the film.

Stage three
Schrödinger's equation for electron waves in atoms

Note for teachers

Most students will have stopped at the end of stage two, and will perhaps have seen the computer film showing the drawing of accurate standing waves, as illustrated in figures 60 to 65. They will not, of course, understand how the calculations are made. But some students could now move to stage three. They can have the 'magic' of the computer removed by doing one solution themselves. The ground has been prepared, and the actual solution is not at all laborious. Presented in the right way, as an effort both to see what the computer did and to see more deeply into the achievement of Schrödinger, the effort could be rewarded by a sense of real achievement. The magnitude of the achievement can hardly be over-emphasized in the classroom. This calculation is one of the giant strides forward in physics. Before it, knowledge of atoms was essentially a heap of facts. After it, scientists felt they *understood* atoms, and were confirmed in that feeling by the power of the method to generate new results. Chemists will be well aware of the repeated use made of the ideas in discussing bonds and orbitals.

An equation for a new dynamics

In stages one and two we used a mixture of old and new ideas. We took kinetic energy and momentum from the physics of Newton, but added the strange and new result, $\lambda = h/mv$, of de Broglie. Put in the right kind of pot, and stirred with the right kind of spoon, these ideas together went some way towards explaining the features of the behaviour of a hydrogen atom which the physics of Newton cannot digest.

If Newton's dynamics will not serve, are there new dynamical equations to be found which will describe the peculiar particle-waves of the quantum world? An answer to this question was provided by Schrödinger. He had to make guesses – leaps in the dark – but by guessing with imagination and skill he produced, among other things, a way of solving the standing-wave problem for atoms. In doing so he was doing more than solving a problem in physics. He turned out to be making a theory of much of chemistry as well.

His equation – when it can be solved – can tell you the energy, size, and structure of any atom you care to think of. The mathematics was formidable, but suddenly physicists could see a way to explain all (or nearly all) of another science. The equation could also be applied to combinations of atoms; to the effects on electrons of having to form wave-patterns with two or more atomic nuclei instead of only one. Then it came out that the theory could also explain the way in which atoms were bonded together, in molecules, and then in solids. The reasons why

---

water H—O has a bond of nearly 90°; why copper atoms, when brought together,
    |
    H

give good conduction whilst silicon atoms do not; why alpha particles with high energy come from nuclei with shorter half-lives than those with low energy – these reasons could all be given by the same basic scheme. A whole vast area had suddenly been made accessible, and it became possible for some to suggest that only the problems of the nucleus and of the stars now remained to be tackled.

In this course, with a little more work, we can follow in the footsteps of Schrödinger and see a little of what he did to make the standing wave idea really predict answers about atoms. We shall see how accurate standing wave patterns can be calculated. It is that understanding – knowing what *kind* of theory it is – which a scientifically educated person might reasonably want to have. Later on in life, if one becomes involved with a science that uses Schrödinger's ideas, one can learn to master and use them. Just now, you should think of yourself as seeing the drama, not expecting to become an actor able to take part yourself.

Schrödinger's equation for standing waves in atoms

Here is one way of writing Schrödinger's equation for calculating the energy levels and size of a hydrogen atom, if the atom is spherical:

$$\frac{d^2A}{dr^2} = -\left(\frac{2\pi}{\lambda}\right)^2 A. \tag{1}$$

Just now, we are simply writing it down, without reasons.

The usual form of Schrödinger's equation

The equation above is not quite like the usual form of Schrödinger's equation. It is the time-independent part of it, usually written:

$$\nabla^2 \psi = -(2\pi)^2 \frac{2m}{h^2}(E-V)\psi.$$

As shown on page 85, for spherical symmetry we can write $A = r\psi$ and

$$\nabla^2(\psi) = \left(\frac{d^2A}{dr^2}\right)\left(\frac{1}{r}\right).$$

The quantity $2m(E-V)$ is the (momentum)^2, and as $mv = h/\lambda$, the equation reduces to:

$$\frac{d^2A}{dr^2} = -\left(\frac{2\pi}{\lambda}\right)^2 A.$$

A stands for the amplitude of a spherical shaped standing wave, the amplitude being different at different radii *r*, as we said in stage two. The value of $A^2 dr$ at any radius *r* is proportional to the chance that an electron will be within the thickness d*r* of a shell of radius *r*, that is, will be found near a distance *r* from the proton. λ is a wavelength, which also depends on *r*. Equation **1** is a rule about waves. To complete it we need to use particle ideas about electrons, to find out how λ should vary with *r*.

In stage two (questions 26 to 29), we saw how the kinetic energy of an electron would vary from place to place. Using the particle rule

total energy E = kinetic energy + potential energy V

we can say

kinetic energy = $E - V$.   **2**

We can now demand that our wave follow a similar rule as it changes wavelength from place to place, since the wavelength λ is given by

$$\lambda = h/mv \qquad \textbf{3}$$

and $mv = \sqrt{2m \text{ (kinetic energy)}}.$ **4**

Thus, using **3** and **4**

$$\lambda^2 = \frac{h^2}{2m \text{ (kinetic energy)}} = \frac{h^2}{2m(E-V)}. \qquad \textbf{5}$$

For any fixed value of *E* we care to choose, we can, if we know the way potential energy *V* varies from place to place, calculate the kinetic energy at each place, and so say how λ must vary from place to place. So the rule of equation **5** tells us at each place what λ must be in equation **1**.

An equation 'out of the blue'?

We have written down Schrödinger's equation (**1**) without justifying it, for a good reason. That is what Schrödinger did. He did not deduce it from something else. He did not write it down to summarize experimental results. He *guessed* what sort of equation to write down.

Two notes of caution

1 Of course, Schrödinger did not guess blindly. Like all good theorists, he knew a lot about what sorts of equations produce particular sorts of results, and so he knew that wave equations produce discrete solutions and integral values. He was also guided by a particular formulation of dynamics, in which quantities like action have maximum or minimum values for the paths a particle actually follows, which did not mention waves, but could be recast into a wave-like equation. The guesswork lay in making these choices; in deciding what to keep from earlier theories, and what to throw away.

2 Not only was the equation a guess: Schrödinger also knew, and we know, that it was almost certainly wrong. For it can be shown to be in conflict with the principles of relativity. As it turned out, Dirac managed to remove this difficulty. But the story carries a nice moral: theoretical physicists are quite prepared to use inexact, guessed principles if they seem to be helpful.

Guessing is commoner in physics than one might suppose.

How else can one go forward if one doesn't know enough to be sure? The difficult art is to guess well, so that one's guess produces answers that agree with experiment.

But Schrödinger did try to make his guess seem fairly plausible. We shall try to do the same, but like him, we cannot prove anything. As we try, some of the magic may be removed from the mathematical symbols.

Why the equation might be plausible

The need is for an equation to represent a standing wave whose wavelength varies with distance *r* as sketched in figure 51.

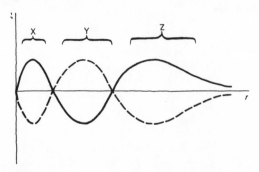

Figure 51

Q42 Put the regions X, Y, and Z in order of decreasing wavelength.

A standing wave of constant wavelength looks like figure 52. The curve may be described by the equation:

$$A = A_0 \sin \frac{2\pi r}{\lambda}.$$

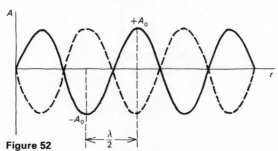

Figure 52

At any distance r, there is an oscillation of amplitude A. The largest value of A is A_0, occurring at intervals $\lambda/2$ apart.

But figure 51 is clearly *not* sinusoidal in form; indeed, this is how one tells that λ varies with r. The sinusoidal function is the very function generated by a constant λ.

If we differentiate the sine equation twice we obtain:

$$\frac{d^2A}{dr^2} = -\left(\frac{2\pi}{\lambda}\right)^2 A.$$

For constant wavelength λ the sine equation is the solution to this differential equation. On a curve, d^2A/dr^2 is represented by how sharply curved the graph is at one place. In earlier graphical solutions (Unit 4, *Waves and oscillations*, using time variations, not distance variations) we used a technique for drawing curves to match changing values of d^2A/dr^2, only then it was d^2A/dt^2.

Figure 53 may remind you of the technique. We drew curves in a number of short steps, previously of size Δt, now of width Δr. Suppose at some stage the curve sloped at some angle like that of the lefthand section of the graph in figure 53. To obtain the next section of graph, the slope may need to be changed. d^2A/dr^2 is the amount by which the slope must change. To draw the curve on, we produce the existing section on at the same slope for a further distance Δr, as shown by the broken line. Then the point at which it cuts the vertical line through the end of the second interval Δr is moved up or down by the amount $(d^2A/dr^2)(\Delta r)^2$. The new segment of graph is drawn passing through this adjusted position.

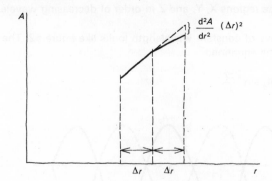

Figure 53

In an equation like

$$\frac{d^2A}{dr^2} = -\left(\frac{2\pi}{\lambda}\right)^2 A$$

the minus sign means that the slope is reduced if A is positive, so keeping the graph curving towards the axis of r. It is the minus sign which generates the to and fro form of the sine or cosine curve. (If the sign were positive, whenever the curve pointed away from the axis, the next bit of curve would point away even more, and the graph would shoot off to infinity. We shall meet that problem with Schrödinger's equation, as it happens.)

Q43 Of the two curves in figure 54, **b** clearly has the smaller wavelength. Which graph is generally more sharply curved?

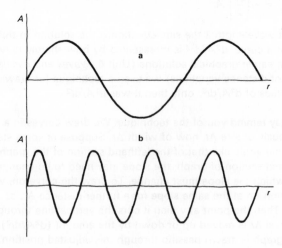

Figure 54

Q44 The equation

$$\frac{d^2A}{dr^2} = -\left(\frac{2\pi}{\lambda}\right)^2 A$$

describes both curves. For which is $2\pi/\lambda$ the greater?

Q45 For which is d^2A/dr^2 greater in magnitude, for the same value of A?

Just because d^2A/dr^2 is greater for **b**, A being the same, **b** turns over in a shorter distance, repeats itself over a shorter distance, and has a shorter wavelength.

Consider the curve in figure 51 again, redrawn in figure 55.

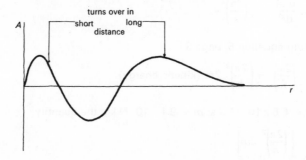

Figure 55

It turns over in a short distance at low values of r, but in a longer distance at larger values of r. It is like a sine curve, but one whose wavelength increases as r increases. Because a sine curve has a constant wavelength, this is *not* a sine curve.

The guess we make about the curve in figure 55 is that it might represent the standing wave in a hydrogen atom, and be the solution of

$$\frac{d^2A}{dr^2} = -\left(\frac{2\pi}{\lambda}\right)^2 A$$

where λ varies from place to place as it must in a hydrogen atom if the rules $\lambda = h/mv$ and kinetic energy $= \frac{1}{2}mv^2$ are obeyed. This, and the decision to trust the energy relationship

kinetic energy = total energy − potential energy

are the essential content of Schrödinger's guess about how to tackle the hydrogen atom problem.

The proof of the pudding

The proof of a theorem in mathematics is in the arguments leading up to it. Schrödinger's equation is not a theorem: it is a guess. It can only be judged by results. Schrödinger showed that it could predict many things. We shall show in detail how it predicts just one thing: the shape of the wave representing the lowest energy level of a hydrogen atom. This will have to stand as a symbol for the many other possible predictions.

Solution for the lowest energy level of hydrogen

Here is equation **1** again:

$$\frac{d^2A}{dr^2} = -\left(\frac{2\pi}{\lambda}\right)^2 A. \tag{1}$$

Also, from equation **5**, page 97,

$$\left(\frac{2\pi}{\lambda}\right)^2 = \left(\frac{2\pi}{h}\right)^2 2m \text{ (kinetic energy)}. \tag{6}$$

With $h = 6.6 \times 10^{-34}$ J s; $m = 9.1 \times 10^{-31}$ kg, the quantity

$$\left[\left(\frac{2\pi}{h}\right)^2 2m\right]$$

comes to $0.165 \times 10^{+39}$ J^{-1} m^{-2}.

You may check this if you wish. Using this value, equation **1** becomes:

$$\frac{d^2A}{dr^2} = -0.165 \times 10^{+39} \text{ (kinetic energy) } A. \tag{7}$$

Equation **7** is the equation whose solution we shall obtain by graphical means. It is suggested that you draw the solution out for yourself, as follows:

The first step

The first step is shown in figure 56. You may use your copy of figure 38, page 79. At $r = 0$, the amplitude A must go to zero, since its square represents the chance per unit shell thickness of finding an electron in the thickness of a shell of radius r; and such a shell vanishes at $r = 0$. The initial slope is arbitrary, and will only affect the size of the curve, not its shape. So we draw a line arbitrarily from $A = 0$ to $A = 1.0$ at $r = 0.1 \times 10^{-10}$ m, as in figure 56.

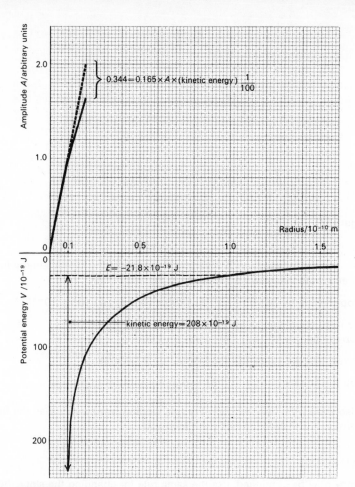

$$0.344 = 0.165 \times A \times (\text{kinetic energy}) \frac{1}{100}$$

$E = -21.8 \times 10^{-19} \text{ J}$

kinetic energy $= 208 \times 10^{-19}$ J

Figure 56
First step – solution of lowest level wave for hydrogen.

At 0.1×10^{-10} m, the kinetic energy can be read off the same graph. It is the distance between the line for E and the curve of the potential energy. Choose $E = -21.8 \times 10^{-19}$ J, the known energy of the lowest level of hydrogen atoms. The kinetic energy after one step is then 208×10^{-19} J, read from figure 56.

The next bit of the graph must not slope so much. It must come down from the projected value of the first bit by $(d^2A/dr^2) (0.1 \times 10^{-10})^2$ since $\Delta r = 0.1 \times 10^{-10}$ m, as in figure 57.

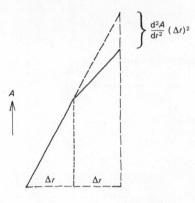

Figure 57

But d^2A/dr^2 is given by equation **7**. Inserting the value of the kinetic energy into equation **7**, and multiplying by $(\Delta r)^2$, we have the instruction,

$$\text{drop the line by } (0.165 \times 10^{+39})\ (208 \times 10^{-19})\ (A)\ (0.1 \times 10^{-10})^2; \qquad \textbf{8}$$

or, the same instruction, cancelling powers of ten,
$$\text{drop the line by } (0.165)\ (A)\ (208)\ (1/100). \qquad \textbf{9}$$

Since A has reached the value 1.0, the instruction **9** becomes

$$\text{drop the line by } (0.165)\ (2.08) = 0.344.$$

Figure 56 also shows the new section of graph, sloping less steeply than the first section, in which this instruction has been followed.

Further steps

The graph may now be continued; use the same rule for changing the slope, but remember to put in the up-to-date values of both the kinetic energy and the amplitude A.

As long as we go on reading the kinetic energy off the graph in units of 10^{-19} J, and r in units of 10^{-10} m, the powers of ten in equation **8** will go on cancelling as in equation **9** so that

$$\text{each new drop} = 0.165\ (\text{previous } A)\ (\text{kinetic energy})\ (1/100).$$

Figure 59 shows the graph continued out to $r = 1.8 \times 10^{-10}$ m. (After $r = 0.8 \times 10^{-10}$ m, the step size can become 0.2, when the factor 1/100 becomes 1/25.)

At about $r = 1.05 \times 10^{-10}$ m, the kinetic energy falls to zero, and the graph is straight. It is not at once clear what should be done beyond this point. If the electron were like a ball rolling up a hill, then at $r = 1.05 \times 10^{-10}$ m its kinetic energy would be zero and it could not roll any further up the hill. If this were true for the electron, A would have to drop to zero for all distances beyond 1.05×10^{-10} m, as in figure 58.

But A cannot suddenly drop to zero in the curve we are drawing, since (d^2A/dr^2) at this point will not then obey the rules. So we can either give up trying to draw a curve at all, or go beyond this point using the rules as if nothing had happened. If we go on, the kinetic energy $(E - V)$ changes sign, so (d^2A/dr^2) changes sign and the curve starts to bend *upwards* in such a way that it comes in gently but steadily to meet the axis.

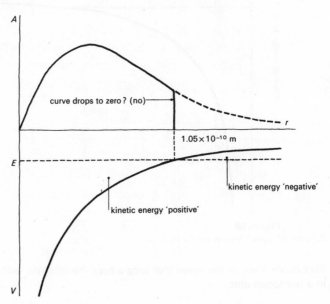

Figure 58

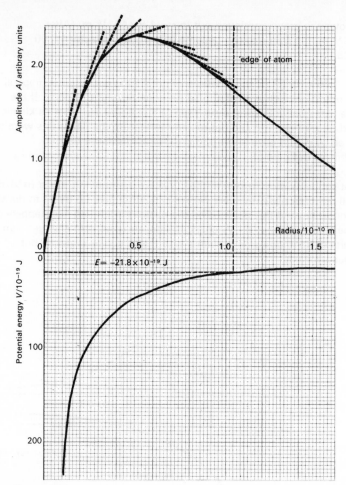

Figure 59
Solution of lowest level wave for hydrogen.

This curve, then, is the wave that tells where the electron will be found most often in a hydrogen atom.

The square of the amplitude drawn represents the chance of finding an electron at each radius within a shell of fixed thickness. The best chance is at radius 0.5×10^{-10} m. This was the radius of the smallest orbit Bohr's theory envisaged. But there is no orbit, just a good chance of finding an electron near that distance. These standing waves that describe the chance of finding an electron are a tenuous kind of reality, but they are the way physicists see the microscopic world. There are no orbits, and no machinery: just waves describing chance. The waves have none of the comfortable ups and downs of a real medium, to make them easy to visualize.

They have properties that are very hard to imagine. Saying, for the wave beyond a certain distance, that the kinetic energy is negative, is preposterous. It means saying that potential energy is greater than the total energy; that the electron can be where it hasn't enough energy to be; that the cow can jump over the moon. Wave ideas suggest to us that we follow this crazy path: it happens often in theoretical physics that an idea which starts by looking quite plain and sensible turns out to invite one into apparently absurd situations. The physicist usually accepts the invitation, to see what will happen. Sometimes an absurd result shows that the theory is wrong, sometimes it turns out to be an important step forward. In the present case, the idea that a particle has a chance of spreading a little beyond where its energy should allow it to go turns out to be an important new idea in physics. In Part Four you may see, for example, how it helps to explain radioactive alpha-decay.

Solving the Schrödinger equation on a computer

In the graphical solution, we took the value of E from experiment, and obtained a curve which tailed down nicely at large values of r, as a boxed-in standing wave must do.

In fact, the equation can locate this and the other energy levels for us, for it is, as we have seen, only at the allowed energy levels that standing waves exist at all. It would be very tedious to draw all the graphs for a wide range of values of E, so as to locate those few which gave good standing wave curves. But a computer is more tolerant, so we have arranged for one to draw the curves on a film whilst it steadily tries out many possible energies E.

The film has three main sequences:

1   At energy $E = -21.8 \times 10^{-19}$ J (the lowest level), the computer repeats the step by step graph drawing shown in figures 56 and 59. This is to show that it is doing just the same as a person can do with pencil and paper.

2   An energy of about -30×10^{-19} J is tried, lower than that of the lowest energy level of hydrogen (-21.8×10^{-19} J). The computer draws a new graph, just as in 1 but more quickly. This graph utterly fails to be a standing wave curve at all. Instead of being 'boxed in', coming down to zero at large radii, it shoots off to infinity instead. Figure 60 is taken from the film, and shows this curve.
Then an energy of about -15×10^{-19} J is tried. This too fails to produce a graph representing a standing wave, as figure 61 shows. The failure this time is of the opposite kind to the previous one; this curve shoots off to minus infinity.
In between the two lies the standing wave for the lowest energy level of hydrogen, at energy -21.8×10^{-19} J, neither going off to infinity in the plus or in the minus direction, but coming down smoothly to the r-axis to represent a wave bounded in space, as any wave representing a stable state of an atom must be.

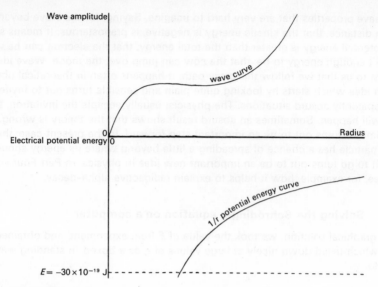

Figure 60
Computer-drawn wave function for hydrogen. Energy about -30×10^{-19} J.

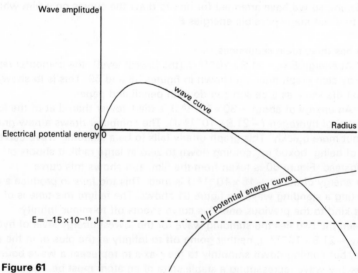

Figure 61
Computer-drawn wave function for hydrogen. Energy about -15×10^{-19} J.

3 Finally, the computer draws the line so quickly that it is all seen at one moment. Then it steadily tries a range of values of E. Generally, after a promising start, the wave goes off to infinity, but at a series of particular values of E, the first being the lowest level -21.8×10^{-19} J, it drops suddenly to the axis and 'fits into a box'.

These good standing waves appear at energies $\dfrac{-21.8 \times 10^{-19}}{4}$ J, $\dfrac{-21.8 \times 10^{-19}}{9}$ J,

and so on, having two, three, etc., loops. At each standing wave, the film 'stops' so that one can look at its shape.

Because the waves occupy a growing space, the scale of r has to be shrunk by a factor of two after each standing wave has been reached. This happens while the standing wave is 'stopped' on the screen. Then the search for the next one begins.

Figures 62 to 65 show the standing waves with one, two, three, and four loops. The horizontal broken lines indicate the energies at which they were found. You can check, if you wish, that these energies are in the ratio 1 to 1/4 to 1/9 to 1/16, measuring each downwards from the axis of r. (The energy scale, unlike the r scale, was not changed during the film.)

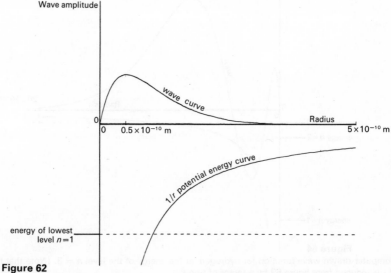

Figure 62
Computer-drawn wave function for hydrogen, at the energy of the lowest level, $n = 1$.
Energy -21.8×10^{-19} J.

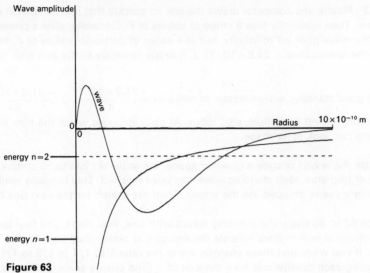

Figure 63
Computer-drawn wave function for hydrogen, at the energy of the level $n = 2$. (Note that the scale of r is reduced from figure 62 by a factor of two.)

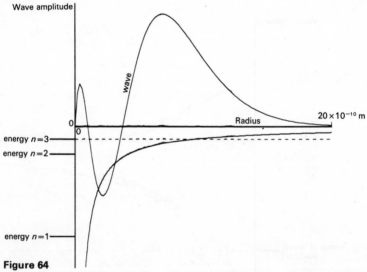

Figure 64
Computer-drawn wave function for hydrogen, at the energy of the level $n = 3$. (Note that the scale of r is reduced from figure 63 by a factor of two.)

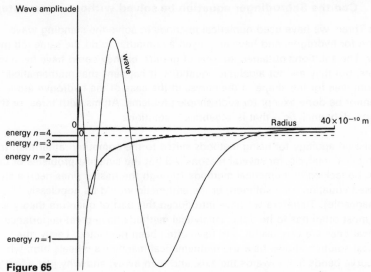

Figure 65
Computer-drawn wave function for hydrogen, at the energy of the level $n = 4$. (Note that the scale of r is reduced from figure 64 by a factor of two.)

The computer-made film of the solution of the wave equation for hydrogen

The film, from which figures 60 to 65 are taken, was made at the request of the Nuffield Advanced Physics project, by the Atlas computer laboratory, Chilton. We are most grateful to the staff of the laboratory for their help and in particular, to Dr F. R. A. Hopgood. The film is published as a film loop as part of the Advanced Physics materials. See page 160.

It is a great advantage to have a projector that can be stopped while projecting an image, so that what is going on in the film at various stages can be pointed out. Some of the crucial points are: **a** When the kinetic energy first goes negative in the first sequence. **b** When the energy E is changed for the first time to a value other than -21.8×10^{-19} J. This is done in close up, the horizontal broken line which indicates the value of E being moved along the axis. **c** When, in the third sequence, E changes continually. **d** When, in the third sequence, a standing wave is first found, and the picture freezes. **e** When the scale of r shrinks by half, immediately after each standing wave has been found. **f** The leaving behind of energy markers on the energy scale at the values where standing waves were found, so ending the film with a ladder of calculated energy levels.

Can the Schrödinger equation be solved without a computer?

In Part Three, we have used numerical methods to solve the standing wave equation for hydrogen, and have employed a computer to do the same job more quickly. The solutions obtained are sets of graphs, or they could have been rows of numbers, but they are not algebraic equations. It happens that mathematicians can write formulae for the shape of the curves in the case of the hydrogen atom, but this cannot be done except for such simple problems. Atoms with three, or thirty, electrons, defy analytic – that is, algebraic – solutions.

We make no apology for using methods suited to the computer rather than to formal mathematical analysis, for several reasons. All but the simplest problems of this sort have to be tackled by numerical methods (though the nastier ones need a start from a guessed equation for a solution, or the arithmetic would be hopelessly unmanageable). Therefore we have introduced this part of quantum theory in the way it most often has to be done. Analytical methods have great importance, but numerical ones are very useful, and have often been neglected. Lastly, the numerical solution shows how the mathematical machine's wheels turn; why the wave curve bends first towards the axis, and then away; and why just a few among many possible curves are bounded in space.

Atoms and mathematics

Why, philosophers have asked, should mathematics ever turn out to describe the real world? What right have we to expect the pure simplicity of equations to fit the messy behaviour of matter? Whatever one's answer to such questions, it is fair to marvel at the way it happens. Quantum theory is yet another example of the way in which mathematics can offer new insight into the world. The art is to know which sort of mathematics to use.

Part Four

The scope of wave mechanics

... The rules of quantum physics are quite definite. People know how to calculate results and how to compare the results of their calculations with experiment. Everyone is agreed on the formalism. It works so well that nobody can afford to disagree with it. But still the picture that we are to set up behind this formalism is a subject of controversy.

'I should like to suggest that one not worry too much about this controversy. I feel very strongly that the stage physics has reached at the present day is not the final stage. It is just one stage in the evolution of our picture of nature, and we should expect this process of evolution to continue in the future. One can be quite sure that there will be better stages simply because of the difficulties that occur in the physics of today.'

P. A. M. Dirac, 'The evolution of the physicist's picture of nature',
Scientific American *Offprint No. 292.*

Aims of Part Four

It is not the aim of this Part to give students any extra information. The aim is to help them to appreciate the scope, value, and power of wave mechanics, by illustrating its use in a variety of contexts.

The series of examples, 1 to 8, may provide teachers with material on which they can draw. A few may find time for most instances, others for only one or two at the level suggested. Still others may prefer to treat all or some much more lightly. Our main concern is that students shall see, or at least hear, that wave mechanics is not limited to hydrogen atoms alone, but commands a great sweep of microscopic physics. Naturally, teachers will hope to call upon the assistance of chemists among the class – indeed a joint session with the chemistry teacher might be very valuable.

Teachers should feel free to simplify or omit material as seems proper to them. A short lecture may be the appropriate medium, or perhaps students should be asked to read selected parts in preparation for a discussion.

Example 1
The helium ion He$^+$

If one wants to understand atoms other than hydrogen, then helium, number two in the Periodic Table, is the next one to try. As with hydrogen, evidence from spectra and ionization experiments should help. The spectrum of ionized helium is shown in figure 66. Ionized helium, one electron and a doubly charged nucleus, is similar enough to hydrogen for simple results to be expected.

The wavelengths, compared with the hydrogen Lyman lines, are shown in table 8.

H (Lyman) $\lambda/10^{-10}$ m	He$^+$ $\lambda/10^{-10}$ m
1216	303
1026	256
972	243
949	237

Table 8
Comparison of wavelengths from H and He$^+$

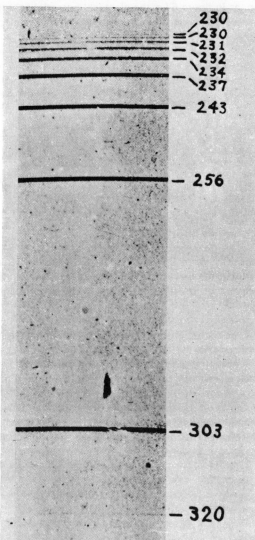

Figure 66
Spectrum of ionized helium. *Photograph, Kruger, P. G. (1930), The physical review, 36, 5, 858.*

Each wavelength for ionized helium He⁺ is just four times smaller than one for the hydrogen atom. It is also the case, as these data suggest, that the lowest energy level for He⁺ has energy -4×13.6 eV, just four times lower than the energy, -13.6 eV, of the lowest level of hydrogen. (In Part Four we shall write all energies in electronvolts. 13.6 eV $= 21.8 \times 10^{-19}$ J.)

It is not hard to see why the helium ion behaves like this.

For hydrogen, as in figure 67 a, the electrical potential energy is given by $e^2/4\pi\varepsilon_0 r$, where e is the value of the charge both on the electron and on the proton.

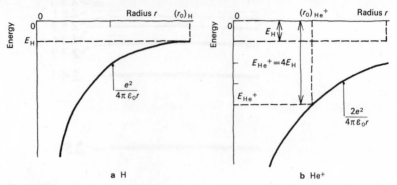

Figure 67
Comparison of energy and radius for H and He$^+$.

The helium ion He$^+$ also has one electron, but has a nucleus with charge $2e$. The potential energy of the electron is given by $2e^2/4\pi\varepsilon_0 r$ as in figure 67 b; a curve of the same form as that for H in figure 67 a, but with the magnitude of every energy value doubled.

How do the sizes of the ions compare? To answer this, we note that a good measure of the 'size' of the atom or ion is the distance r_0 at which the total energy E is equal to the potential energy. At r_0, the electron has no kinetic energy at all; except in wave mechanics, the electron cannot be more than r_0 from the nucleus.

As figure 67 shows, $(r_0)_H$ must be twice $(r_0)_{He^+}$, since halving the radius and doubling the charge will quadruple the potential energy, which is just what the spectral data say must happen. In terms of the equations for the two values of r_0:

$$4(E)_H = 4\left[\frac{e^2}{4\pi\varepsilon_0 (r_0)_H}\right] = (E)_{He^+} = \frac{2e^2}{4\pi\varepsilon_0 (r_0)_{He^+}}$$

so

$$\frac{(r_0)_H}{(r_0)_{He^+}} = 2.$$

The standing wave which describes the one electron in the helium ion must have one loop in the lowest state, as for hydrogen, but must fit into half the space, so its wavelength must be half that for the electron in the hydrogen atom.

But the change to the wavelength is already decided, through the relationship $\lambda = h/mv$ and the energy. If we suppose, as before (page 91) that the mean kinetic energy is proportional to the total energy E, then

$$\lambda \propto \frac{1}{\sqrt{E}} \qquad \text{(since } mv \propto \sqrt{\text{kinetic energy}}\text{)}.$$

E has quadrupled; the wavelength must have halved. So on both counts the new wavelength fits. He$^+$ has a larger energy for the lowest level both because of the stronger pull of the doubly charged nucleus, and because an He$^+$ ion is half as big as an H atom.

Algebraic version

$E \propto Z/r_0$, from rules for calculating the electrical potential energy, where Z is the number of protons in the nucleus.

But $\lambda \propto r_0$, and $\lambda \propto 1/\sqrt{E}$ if $E \propto$ mean kinetic energy.

So combining the above equations, $E \propto Z\sqrt{E}$
or $E \propto Z^2$.

If Z goes from 1 to 2, E is quadrupled, as the spectral data confirm.

Example 2
Explaining X-ray spectra

The hydrogen Lyman lines and the ultra-violet spectral lines from He$^+$ discussed in example 1 above are the shortest wavelength lines these atoms emit. Other atoms higher in the Periodic Table also emit short wave radiation: X-rays.

The X-rays are produced when an electron which was in a deep energy level, close to the nucleus, has been ejected previously, and is replaced by another 'falling' into this deep level and emitting energy.

The energy E emitted is equal to the energy of the level, and, being emitted as a photon of frequency f, the frequency is given by

$$E = hf.$$

But also $E \propto Z^2$ from example 1 above, if Z is the number of charges on the nucleus of the atom involved, and the energy level concerned contains an electron very near the nucleus, with no other electrons closer to the nucleus to complicate matters.

Thus, if the frequency f of the shortest X-ray wavelength emitted by atoms is measured, for atoms with different nuclear charges, we should find that:

$$f \propto Z^2$$
or $\quad \sqrt{f} \propto Z.$

Figure 68 shows such a plot of $\sqrt{f}$ against Z, using data obtained by Moseley, who was the first to test this relationship.

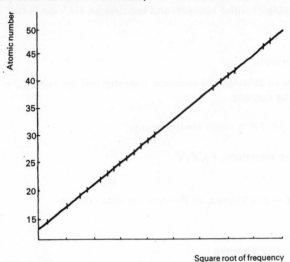

Figure 68
X-ray frequencies and atomic number Z.
After Moseley, H. G. J. (1913) Philosophical Magazine (6), **27**, *1024.*

Notes to teachers

1 The argument above is no more than suggestive, but was not meant to be rigorous. In particular, $\sqrt{f}$ is actually proportional to $Z-1$ more nearly, because of the screening effect on the nuclear charge of the other electron sharing the level involved. The PSSC text, *College physics*, Chapter 35, gives a good account of X-ray spectra and screening effects.
2 Moseley's original writings on X-ray spectra and their implications for understanding the Periodic Table are reproduced in *Classical scientific papers – physics*, from page 182. The passage on page 189, discussing the evidence for the Periodic Table as a sequence in order of increasing nuclear charge, is especially interesting.

Example 3
The helium–lithium jump

The Periodic Table has the striking feature that at intervals, an increase of one more proton in the nucleus produces a dramatic change in chemical properties. For instance, He → Li, Ne → Na, A → K. We can understand a little about this too.

Consider neutral helium, with two electrons. The energy needed to remove one electron (ionization energy) is 24.6 eV. This is less than the value 4×13.6 eV for He$^+$, because the negative charge on each of the two electrons somewhat reduces the attraction of the nucleus for the other. (Each electron 'sees' the nucleus partly shielded by the negative charge of the other electron.) It is as if the nucleus had an effective charge between 1 and 2 units, so far as each electron is concerned.

Consider the lithium nucleus with $Z = 3$. Following the $E \propto Z^2$ rule, an ionization energy of 9×13.6 eV might be expected. Even if the other two electrons shielded the third as well as possible, making Z effectively equal to 1, the energy would be at least 13.6 eV. The experimental value is much less, only 5.4 eV, this easily removed electron producing the high reactivity of lithium. By contrast, helium atoms seem reluctant to lose or gain an electron, and helium is unreactive.

The third electron also occupies more space than might be expected. In lithium metal, the atom seems to have a radius of about 1.51×10^{-10} m. In an ionic crystal, like LiF, the Li$^+$ ion with one electron missing has a radius of only 0.68×10^{-10} m. See figure 69.

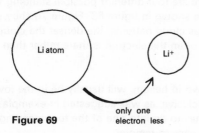

Li atom

Li$^+$

only one
electron less

Figure 69

The only explanation is that this third electron is not in the lowest energy level, $n = 1$, at all, but is in a higher level. $n = 2$ seems likely. The energy will be lower by the Balmer $1/n^2$ rule.

If the effective value of Z were 1, the energy should be $\dfrac{13.6}{2^2} = 3.4$ eV.

This is nearly right – and since it is possible that the effective value of Z is more than 1, since the two inner electrons will not provide a perfect shield – it is easy to see how 5.4 eV can be explained.

To remove a second electron from lithium, that is to change from Li$^+$ to Li^{++}, requires 75.6 eV; this must be from the $n = 1$ state, for which energy would be 122.4 eV for no shielding, and 54.4 eV for perfect shielding (effective value of $Z = 2$).

The third electron does not go into the same state as the first two. A systematic look at ionization potentials shows several 'jumps' like this one (see Unit 5); each 'jump' can be explained by saying that no more than two electrons can go into any one of the standing wave patterns – the extra electron in an atom with one more proton has to go into a wave state of different energy.

This is a simple version of the 'exclusion principle', first suggested by Pauli. Electrons are not gregarious; they 'want to be alone'.

Example 4
The number patterns 2–8–8–18, and so on, in the Periodic Table

So far we have only considered standing waves in hydrogen which have spherical symmetry; that is, the electron is equally likely to be found in any direction.

Not all the possible standing waves for hydrogen are like this. For the lowest energy level, $n = 1$, at -13.6 eV, there is only one possible standing wave, which is the one drawn out in Part Three, stage three (see figures 59 and 62). But for the next level, $n = 2$, energy $-(13.6/2^2)$ eV, there are four different possible standing waves, only one of which is the symmetrical one shown in figure 63. Figure 70 shows another way of representing the waves, as cloud patterns; the denser the cloud the larger the wave amplitude and the more often the electron is there rather than elsewhere.

The one electron in hydrogen, and the two in helium, will usually be in the lowest energy state, $n = 1$. But electrons are exclusive, as was suggested in example 3 above, and the third electron in lithium has to go into one of the four standing waves of higher energy, and is therefore easy to remove.

Each of these four waves can have two electrons so there is no further dramatic drop in ionization energy until $2+8$ electrons have been put in: at the 11th electron a higher state, $n = 3$, has to be used. The periodic repeats at 2–8–8–18–18 seen in many physical properties (see Unit 5) can all be understood just by calculating orbitals (the chemist's name for the standing wave patterns) and giving two electrons to each.

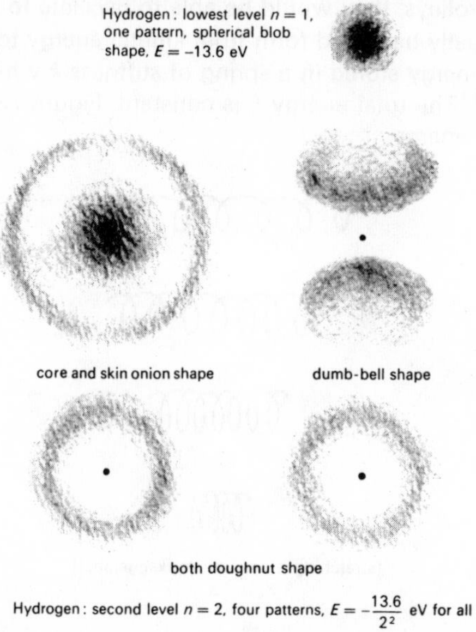

Hydrogen: lowest level $n = 1$, one pattern, spherical blob shape, $E = -13.6$ eV

core and skin onion shape

dumb-bell shape

both doughnut shape

Hydrogen: second level $n = 2$, four patterns, $E = -\frac{13.6}{2^2}$ eV for all

Figure 70

Some states of the hydrogen atom. For $n = 1$, there is one spherically symmetric state. For $n = 2$, there are four states; only one being spherically symmetric. The density of shading in the figure represents the chance that a small volume nearby will be occupied by an electron. That is, the density represents ψ^2, where $\psi^2 dv$ is the chance that an electron will occupy volume dv. Note that previous graphs of spherically symmetric states (figures 59 and 62 to 65) plotted not ψ, but $A = r\psi$, so that $A^2 dr = r^2\psi^2 dr$ is proportional to the chance that an electron will occupy a spherical shell of radius r, thickness dr, and volume $4\pi r^2 dr$. $A = r\psi$ for the ground state has a maximum at the Bohr radius, but the function ψ for the same state is greatest at the nucleus. The maximum arises because, although ψ^2, the chance per unit volume, decreases with r, the volume $4\pi r^2 dr$ of a spherical shell increases with volume.

Example 5
Oscillating molecules with equally spaced energy levels

Both physicists and chemists are interested in studying the bonds between molecules, how strong they are, or how easily they stretch or bend. Wave mechanics helps them to obtain such information from measurements of the frequencies at which bonded molecules absorb or emit radiation as they oscillate.

For instance, the two iodine atoms in the molecule I_2 behave rather as if they were connected by a spring of nearly constant stiffness k, as suggested in figure 71.

Figure 71

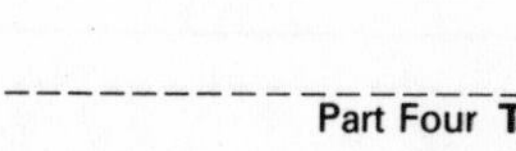

If the atoms were, say, trolleys, they would be able to oscillate to and fro, their energy changing continually back and forth from kinetic energy to potential energy (Unit 4). The potential energy stored in a spring of stiffness k which is stretched by an extra length x is $\frac{1}{2}kx^2$. The total energy E is constant. Figure 72 illustrates the changes of position and energy.

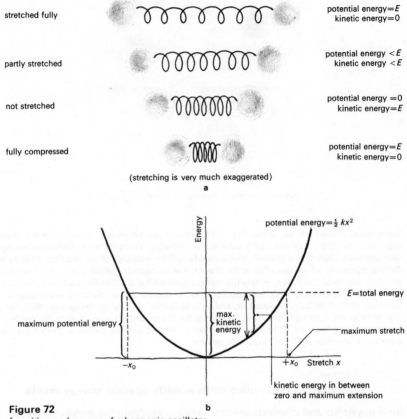

Figure 72
Changes of position and energy of a harmonic oscillator.

For atomic sized objects, the wave behaviour of particles is important. As with electrons, the amplitude of a wave decides how likely it is that the atoms will be a certain distance apart. As an approximation, we suppose that the atoms will not move in and out more than a distance x_0, the maximum stretch, where $E = \frac{1}{2}kx_0^2$.

The standing wave, wave length λ, which says where the atoms may be, must fit into a space of size about x_0. If the standing wave has n loops, then

$$n\lambda \propto x_0$$

for the standing wave to fit in a 'box' of size x_0.

For the lowest level, $n = 1$, for the next, $n = 2$, and so on. The energy E of each level fits a very simple pattern: the energy increases in equal steps as n increases. The energy levels are equally spaced. Indeed, this fact was used in Unit 9, *Change and chance*, in the discussion of the model of a solid imagined as being made up of many harmonically oscillating atoms. It is not hard to see how this result comes about, as follows.

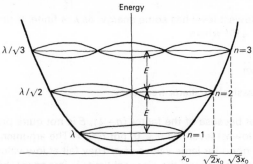

Figure 73
Waves fitting into a harmonic oscillator 'energy well'.

Figure 73 suggests how the waves for $n = 1$, 2, and 3 might fit into the 'box' formed by the harmonic oscillator.

The kinetic energy is always between zero and E; suppose the mean kinetic energy is proportional to E. Then, since the mean momentum mv is proportional to the square root of the mean kinetic energy,

$$\text{mean momentum} \propto \sqrt{E}$$

Thus   mean wavelength $\lambda \propto 1/\sqrt{E}$ since $\lambda = h/mv$.

But for the harmonic oscillator,

$$\text{maximum amplitude } x_0 \propto \sqrt{E} \qquad \text{since } E = \tfrac{1}{2}kx_0^2.$$

Using these results for λ and x_0 in the equation for waves in a box

$$n\lambda \propto x_0$$

we have $n(1/\sqrt{E}) \propto \sqrt{E}$

or $n \propto E$.

So the energy E increases in equal steps as the number n increases.

Further details for teachers

1 *Average kinetic energy*

Average kinetic energy $= \displaystyle\int_0^{x_0} (E - \tfrac{1}{2}kx^2)\, dx \Big/ \int_0^{x_0} dx = E/3$.

2 The lowest level has some energy, as λ is finite. It turns out that $E = (n + \tfrac{1}{2})hf$ where

$$f = \frac{1}{2\pi}\sqrt{\frac{k}{m}}$$

is the classical oscillator frequency.

Note that because of the factor $(n + \tfrac{1}{2})$, E is not quite proportional to n, and the lowest level has $n = 0$, not $n = 1$. The arguments of page 122 are only good for large values of n. They fail at low values of n, because the spreading beyond the classical limits is important there. Indeed, for $n = 0$, the spreading is all-important, and yields the lowest state, energy $\tfrac{1}{2}hf$.

The wave for the lowest level has one maximum at $x = 0$, so the atoms are most likely to be at their equilibrium distance. It is the quantum analogue of an oscillator at rest. For large n, the wave looks like figure 74. The amplitude turns out to be larger for large displacements, corresponding to the classical oscillator, which spends most time at large displacements, where it is moving slowly. The wave tails off exponentially beyond the classical limits $\pm x_0$.

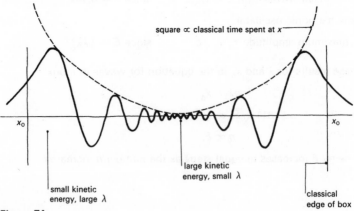

Figure 74
Harmonic oscillator, large n.

3 The levels for real oscillating molecules become more closely spaced as the energy E rises. A typical potential well is shown in figure 75.

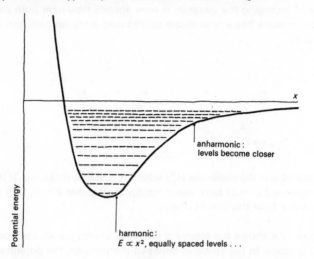

Figure 75

anharmonic:
levels become closer

harmonic:
$E \propto x^2$, equally spaced levels . . .

Near to equilibrium, for low energy levels, the well is harmonic. But as E rises, the well expands more than proportionately to x^2, the wavelengths do not diminish so rapidly with E, and thus the levels rise in smaller steps.

Example 6
How a molecule is held together

The idea that electrons have wave properties is the basis for understanding how some atoms cling together to form molecules. The simplest molecule to think about is the ion of molecular hydrogen H_2^+, made of two protons sharing one electron.

The following account is much influenced by PSSC *College physics*, page 663. Teachers may find the PSSC version briefer, better, or both.

Figure 76 *a* shows a proton H⁺ separate from a hydrogen atom. Figure 76 *b* shows the same, but the electron is bound to the other proton. Figure 76 *c* shows another way of arranging the electron. It now spends time near both protons, and the electron wave has a new shape spread over a region near and between the two protons.

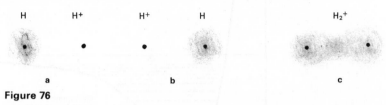

Figure 76

Figure 76 *c* is the molecule H_2^+, which is a stable molecule. If it is stable, the arrangement *c* must have lower energy than either *a* or *b*. It is possible to explain in outline how this comes about.

Figure 77 *a* shows the electrical potential energy for an electron produced by the two protons. In the space in between the protons, the potentials may be added to give the hump shown in figure 77 *b*.

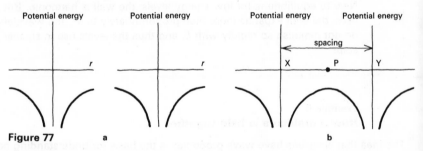

Figure 77

The problem then is to fit an electron wave into this new type of box. A good first guess at a possible answer is to just add the two electron waves which fit the two boxes separately – they will fit near the two nuclei, around X, Y, but not around P – here some adjustment will be needed to make the answer fit. Such adjustment gives a new wave, looking like the one shown in figure 76 *c*. The energy is lower than that for figure 76 *a* or *b* for two reasons:

1 The wave has bigger amplitude in the space between the two nuclei so the electron has more chance to be attracted electrically by both of them, which gives a lower potential energy.

2 At the same time, because the 'box' of figure 77 *b* is bigger than that around a single nucleus, the wave can have a bigger wavelength, and therefore the values of momentum, and so of kinetic energy, can be lower.

The molecule is thus more stable than either of the alternatives because the total energy is lower. The ionization potential of H_2^+ is 16.3 eV compared with 13.6 eV for H.

Other molecules

The same principles apply to other molecules, but the problems are usually more complicated. For the H_2 molecule, which is also stable, a very similar wave to that shown in figure 76 c fits the box, though the box is modified by the electrical effects of the extra electron.

If we try to add more electrons, and make, say, H_3 or HeH, or He_2, the rule that only two electrons may occupy a wave state comes into play, and the extra electron or electrons have to occupy other wave states. It turns out that the other waves do not give the electrons a high chance of being at places like P in figure 77 b, where their potential energy is low, so these molecules are either much less stable, like He_2, or do not exist at all, like HeH.

The above is a small part of a larger story. There are three main ideas in it:
   1   Fitting waves into more complicated boxes.
   2   Allowing for the changes in electrical energy.
   3   Obeying the rule of not more than two electrons for each wave state.

These rules, taken together, are the key to understanding the bonds which cement together the common molecules, and many solids. These electron-sharing bonds are known as covalent bonds.

Example 7
The water molecule

Water is made of one oxygen and two hydrogen atoms. X-ray studies indicate that the molecule has the form O—H, with a right angle (nearly) between the O—H

|
H

bonds. Wave ideas can explain this.

The peculiar behaviour of water – high melting and boiling points, great power to dissolve things – depends largely on the molecule being lopsided, or 'polar'. If water did not behave like this, but behaved like, say, H_2S, life as we know it would be impossible.

The electron standing waves for oxygen not only depend on distance from the nucleus but also vary with direction. Similar effects may be seen in two dimensions, with Chladni plates or rubber diaphragms (see page 67). In Figure 78 a, we have shaded the region where the wave is fairly large. It has four lobes sticking out into space round the nucleus.

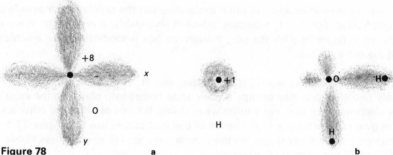

Figure 78 a b
Electron cloud, for oxygen, hydrogen, and water.

Figure 78 a shows two separate electron waves for oxygen which we have labelled the x and y waves because they point along two directions at right angles. If an H atom is brought up, the H wave and the oxygen x wave can be combined to give a new wave of lower energy, and two electrons (one from H, one from the O) can occupy this wave state. See Figure 78 b.

Another H can similarly be brought up to share the y wave. The result is H_2O. Because the x and y waves for oxygen are at right angles, the angle between the O—H bonds is almost a right angle.

Knowledge about the angular patterns of standing waves fits in with measurements we can make on the angular shapes of molecules. The whole architecture of molecules is related to the standing wave patterns which can be fitted in the three-dimensional box of an inverse square law field.

In Unit 1 the angle between bonds in the rubber molecule was mentioned. This angle arises for similar reasons. Chemists in the class may know of other interesting instances. Graphite, met in Part Two of this Unit, is one.

Example 8
Alpha decay

Alpha particles from a radioactive substance can be fired at nuclei of that same substance, in experiments similar to Rutherford's alpha-scattering experiment, performed by Geiger and Marsden (Unit 5). Such alpha particles rebound from the electrical 'wall' around the nucleus. That is, they approach a nucleus until their electrical potential energy is as big as their original kinetic energy, which might be about 5 MeV. Then they move away again, running 'downhill' until, at a large distance, when their potential energy is zero again, they have got back their original kinetic energy.

The puzzle is, how could the alpha particles ever have got out of the nucleus in the first place, with 5 MeV of energy? If they rebound from the electrical wall, the wall *must* rise above 5 MeV, to some place like X in figure 79. So alpha particles which emerged with 5 MeV energy must be trapped inside the nucleus, behind X, and they are trapped forever, or so it seems, since they have not the energy to climb over the hill whose peak is at X. If they could get over the hill, then when they arrived at an identical nucleus in a scattering experiment, they could reach the hill top again, and many would drop inside the nucleus. They do not do so, so the difficulty remains.

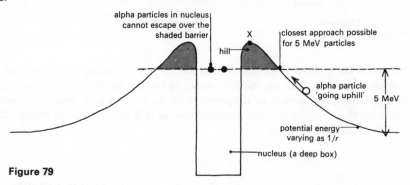

Figure 79

Wave mechanics provides the clue to the puzzle. In all of figures 62–65, showing waves for the hydrogen atom, the wave leaks into places where a particle ought not to be, because the particle has not enough energy to be there. These are the regions at large radius where the potential energy is greater than the total energy, so that the kinetic energy would be negative.

In such regions the wave exists, but dies away rapidly. Now the hill, shown shaded in figures 79 and 80, over which the alpha particles cannot climb on our previous argument, is just such a region. Inside the box representing the nucleus the alpha particles must be described by trapped standing waves. But, as suggested in figure 80, these waves can leak out of the box if they die away under the hill, but the hill has only a limited thickness, so that just a little wave amplitude is left outside the hill.

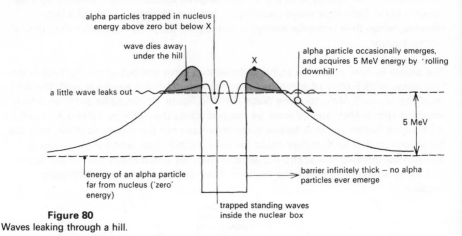

Figure 80
Waves leaking through a hill.

If there is some wave amplitude outside the hill, there is some chance that an alpha particle will turn up outside the hill instead of staying inside forever. It turns up with energy 5 MeV above zero, as suggested in figure 80, and runs down the electrical potential slope, converting this potential energy to 5 MeV of kinetic energy. We say that the nucleus has decayed.

A complication. It was not quite true to imply above that all alpha particles fired at a similar parent nucleus rebound. If some can tunnel out, a similar proportion can tunnel *in*. The effect is very small but it has been observed.

The larger the alpha particle energy, the thinner the hill it has to escape through, and the greater the wave amplitude outside will be, having died away less under the hill. So nuclei with high energy alpha decays should release alpha particles more often, and have short half-lives. This turns out to be true. Figure 81 illustrates the idea. A stable nucleus will be one for which the alpha particles in the nucleus lie at an energy below zero, so that the wall is infinitely thick, and no waves escape.

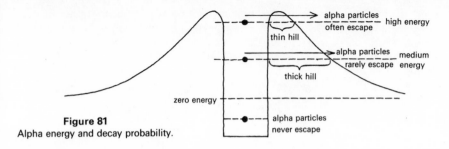

Figure 81
Alpha energy and decay probability.

The effect is called 'tunnelling'. It is not confined to radioactive decay. An electronic device called a 'tunnel diode' uses the same effect, some of the current it passes being carried by electrons which have 'tunnelled' through a potential hill inside the device.

The escape of an alpha particle from a nucleus is a matter of chance, for the wave which is found outside the hill only describes the chance of finding a particle outside. It is for this reason that radioactive decay is a random process. Radioactive decay was the first example of a random process contained in the course, in Unit 5. Now we see that this randomness is related to the randomness that lies very deep in physics: the chance-like nature of the waves of wave mechanics.

Postscript

A personal note on the origin and future of quantum mechanics
by Professor Sir Nevill Mott
Cavendish Professor of Experimental Physics,
University of Cambridge

The organizers of the Advanced Physics Project have asked me to write a few words about quantum mechanics, both as it looked forty years ago when I started research and as it looks now. Forty years ago Bohr's theory of the atom held the field. We were brought up on it, our textbooks and lectures contained beautiful pictures of elliptical orbits, and I think we students really believed they existed. They explained so much: the Balmer series in the spectrum of hydrogen, X-ray spectra, and a lot more besides.

I believe that the leaders of physics at that time were divided into those who were trying to make the Bohr theory better and better and those — many fewer — who felt it would in the end have to be replaced by something quite different. Among the latter was the German physicist Heisenberg and he and others produced the first breakthrough, the so-called 'matrix mechanics' which did promise to be quite general. It promised to be a form of mechanics replacing Newtonian mechanics, capable of answering any question that Newtonian mechanics could answer but of giving different answers at any rate for problems about atoms. The mathematics promised to be difficult; physicists who were good at mathematics thought they would have a lot of fun.

Schrödinger's equation was a bit of a bombshell. Schrödinger used 'easy' mathematics, differential equations, which are part of any university course. I remember a talented mathematical contemporary saying to me, 'all the fun has gone out of quantum theory, I'm going to study Law' — and he did. He was wrong; the later developments of quantum mechanics are difficult enough in all conscience. But what I remember most vividly about this equation was that Schrödinger himself did not know what it meant! He thought his 'wave intensity' must be interpreted as density of charge. We know now that this is only true in a statistical sense, and that the amplitude gives the *probability* that a particle will be found somewhere. This was first clearly stated by Max Born, a German physicist who moved to England in 1933.

To start research just after Schrödinger's equation was — perhaps — like being an explorer just after Columbus. The facts of physics and chemistry were wide open. In a very few years Schrödinger's equation was used to explain why atoms form molecules, why some solids conduct electricity and others do not, how radioactive decay occurs, and the details of the spectra of helium and most other atoms. It did everything that Bohr's theory could do and a lot more. Most convincing of all, it made predictions. For instance, it showed that the Rutherford scattering formula — really the basis of all of nuclear physics — did not work if an alpha particle hit a nucleus, namely of helium, of just the same kind as itself. When this prediction was made, the Cavendish Laboratory quickly mounted the experiments which showed that it was so. And even more important, quantum mechanics predicted that moving protons, quite slow by the standards of nuclear physics, could penetrate into an atomic nucleus of a light element, and so encouraged Cockcroft and Walton to make their famous first disintegration of the nucleus with artificially accelerated particles.

What quantum mechanics did *not* do was to predict the neutron! And if one looks at quantum mechanics as it is today, it is in nuclear or particle physics that it is still floundering. Here it is just like Bohr's theory was, brilliantly successful sometimes, failing at others, constantly being modified, and calling on all the techniques of advanced mathematics. No one would pretend that here it was the last word.

But outside the nucleus, the least one can say is that no one has proved it wrong. In the theory of molecules the theoretical chemists use all the resources of modern computers to calculate the properties of molecules and achieve greater and greater success. Schrödinger's equation gets more and more complicated as the number of electrons in a molecule increases, so the computer comes into its own here. In solids, particularly metals, there are problems of real mathematical difficulty. Superconductivity is one, understood in principle but not in detail. Our whole thinking about semiconductors and transistors is based on quantum mechanics and has become a very exact branch of science. At the time of writing there is a great deal of interest in non-crystalline semiconductors, which present a more difficult problem — how does the electron find its way among a jumble of molecules put together anyhow? But no one doubts that quantum mechanics is competent to give the answer.

What of the future? I see quantum mechanics applied to more and more complicated systems — the molecules of biology, technically useful alloys, conducting glasses, and polymers. Quantum mechanics, I dare guess, will not change, but the methods of using it will change as they have already in the last decade or two. And in the nucleus and in stellar interiors, it would be arrogant to guess. Will a billion dollar accelerator give us the final understanding of the nuclear particles, or will some brilliant insight in theory? Only the future can show.

Appendix

The Compton effect: a photo-electric game of billiards

If there is time for it (at least two periods) the Compton effect may strengthen the impression that photons can behave like particles. In the Compton effect, photons rebound from electrons, and it is found that the laws of conservation of energy and momentum applied to the collisions predict the angles and energies of the photon and the electron after the collision. The analysis suggested below is rudimentary: fuller versions may be found in many texts. The following are suitable for students:

Born, *The restless Universe*, page 133.

Project Physics, *Text, Unit 5*.

Rogers, *Physics for the inquiring mind*, page 727.

In 1923, Arthur Compton discovered that photons could bounce off particles like electrons, in collisions which were very similar to collisions between particles. He found how to play billiards with light. It is possible to repeat a simplified version of the experiment in the school laboratory. The effect is best seen with the very energetic, and very particle-like, gamma ray photons from a radioactive source.

Optional demonstration
10.10 The Compton effect

- 130/1   scaler
- 130/3   GM tube holder
- 130/6   gamma GM tube
- 195/1   pure gamma source
- 1069   apparatus for showing the Compton effect (see figure 82)
- 512/2   beaker, 400 cm³

Practical details

The apparatus, shown in figure 82, can easily be made in a school, though casting the lead cylinder and forming its end into a cone are a little troublesome. The lead cylinder is 60 mm tall, and about 20 mm in diameter, the lower end being turned down to about 15 mm diameter, or a little larger than the diameter of the source.

The lead sheet is 1 mm thick, with a hole in the middle cut to take the smaller end of the lead cylinder. The hole should be smaller than the wide end of the cylinder, so that the sheet can rest on the cylinder in the last part of the experiment, as in figure 84.

The shape of the cylinder is intended to cover the whole end face of the counter in the first part of the experiment, so reducing as much as possible the number of photons reaching the counter except via the scattering material. The end with reduced diameter allows a greater flux of photons into the scattering material than a wide-ended cylinder would do.

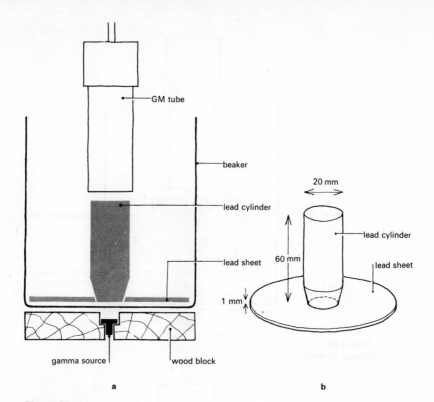

Figure 82
Apparatus for showing the Compton effect.
a Arrangement of apparatus.
b Lead cylinder and lead sheet.

The geometry is intended to favour as large a flux of scattered photons into the counter as possible, regardless of the angle of scatter, as long as this angle is substantial. The counter is placed so as to discriminate in favour of scattered photons, because it is insensitive to photons entering its end face, but sensitive to those entering its sides. An end window counter such as the MX 168 will not do, since it has shielded walls, and the soft scattered gamma rays are unlikely to enter the counter at all.

The source is placed, facing upwards, in a hole drilled in a disc of wood so that its surface is about 5 mm below the top of the wood. The wood requires a hole of large diameter to be sunk into it a little way, to take the body of the source, with a 4 mm hole drilled deeper in the centre, to take the 4 mm pin on the back of the source.

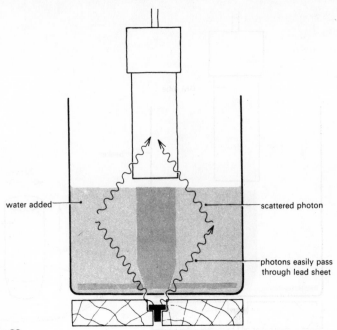

Figure 83
Photons scattered by water.

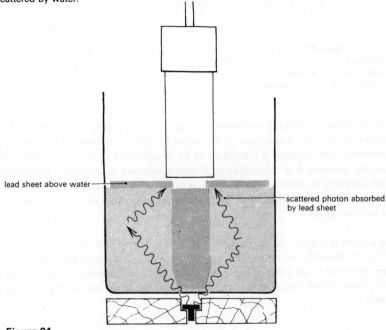

Figure 84
Demonstration that the scattered photons are 'soft'.

With the apparatus arranged as in figure 82, the number of gamma ray photons reaching the GM tube through the cylinder, plus any background, is counted over a period of five minutes. A count of about 600 may be expected. Subsidiary, rather tedious experiments, would show that the lead sheet and the glass beaker have a negligible effect on this count. It will probably be best to avoid making these tests.

Water is now poured into the beaker, up to the top of the lead cylinder. Take care not to disturb the positions of the cylinder, GM tube, or source, and not to wet the last two. Make a further five-minute count. The count is now larger, perhaps 800, or more if the photon flux and the scattering geometry are optimized. The increase should certainly be four or more standard deviations larger than the previous count, so the change is not likely to be a random fluctuation.

One may now argue that the extra scattered photons must, from the geometry, have been turned through a substantial angle. An argument, indicated below, suggests that the scattered photons will now have lower momentum, longer wavelength, and less energy, and should pass less readily through lead on that account. To test this, lift the lead sheet from the bottom of the beaker, and rest it on top of the cylinder, taking care to restore the cylinder and counter to their former positions over the source. A final five-minute count now shows that the number of photons reaching the counter has fallen to a value differing little, if at all, from its first value. No, or practically no scattered photons penetrate the lead sheet, though their parent photons managed it easily.

Water is a convenient scattering material, and costs no more than a beaker to hold it. The same volume of wood (with a central hole drilled to take the lead cylinder) is no better, so far as we can tell. Aluminium might be better, but a suitably shaped lump would be expensive. Perspex could also be tried, again at some expense.

Collisions of photons

We imagine the extra gamma rays counted with the water present to have been scattered through a substantial angle, as suggested in figure 85. Were this an ordinary collision between particles, one would wish to know the energy and momentum of the incoming particle.

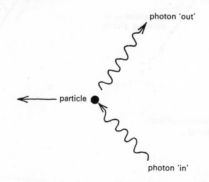

Figure 85

The energy of gamma rays from Co^{60} is 1.2 MeV, of the order 2×10^{-13} J. Were the photons particles, of kinetic energy $\frac{1}{2}mv^2$, velocity v, their momentum mv would be

$$\frac{2}{v} \times \text{(kinetic energy)}.$$

The gamma rays travel at velocity 3×10^8 m s^{-1}. For an order of magnitude of their momentum, we take

$$\text{momentum} = \frac{\text{energy}}{\text{velocity}} = \frac{2 \times 10^{-13}}{3 \times 10^8} \approx 10^{-21} \text{ kg m s}^{-1}.$$

(Actually, the factor $\frac{1}{2}$ in $\frac{1}{2}mv^2$ comes from classical mechanics. In relativity, it vanishes for photons, and the relation

$$\text{momentum} = \frac{\text{energy}}{\text{velocity}}$$

is exact.)

If momentum is conserved in the collision, which one cannot suppose it to be without evidence, the only way for the photon to be turned through a substantial angle is for the electron to carry off substantial sideways momentum. This remark applies to photons the rules for ordinary particles. Figure 86 sketches some sort of possible momentum diagram. We know little except that the electron must acquire momentum not substantially less than the original momentum of the photon, if the scattering angle is more than slight. Perhaps the momentum carried off might be estimated at 3×10^{-22} kg m s^{-1}.

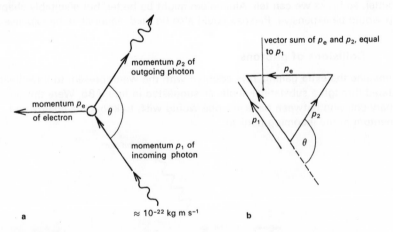

Figure 86
a Momenta in a photon–electron collision.
b Adding the momenta vectorially.

If the particle that scattered the photon was a massive nucleus, it could have carried off momentum without recoiling at high velocity with great kinetic energy. In general, the particle the photon strikes will acquire kinetic energy given by

$$\text{kinetic energy} = \frac{(\text{momentum})^2}{2(\text{mass})}.$$

The momentum is more or less fixed, so the energy carried off is larger the smaller the mass of the struck particle. If the particle is an electron, its mass is only 10^{-30} kg which, with the momentum estimate of the order of 3×10^{-22} kg m s^{-1}, gives an estimate in the region of 5×10^{-14} J, or a little less than 0.5 MeV, for the energy the electron will carry off.

Thus, an electron struck by a 1 MeV photon may carry off a good part of the photon's energy, and photons scattered through a substantial angle should have considerably reduced energy, and so have a longer wavelength. They will pass less easily through lead, and the last part of the experiment tests this point. Better experiments set out to measure the exact change of wavelength predicted by more precise versions of the theory, with favourable results.

(Detailed attempts to work from equations of energy and momentum conservation are not necessary to make the point required, and they could give absurd answers — showing the energy of the electron to be greater than the initial photon energy, for example — if non-relativistic formulae are used.)

More questions

Q1 This question can be answered from two points of view: knowing about the electromagnetic wave theory of light; and knowing about the dual photon-wave description of light.

Hertz, who was the first man deliberately to manufacture electromagnetic waves in the laboratory in a test of the electromagnetic wave theory of Maxwell, is reputed to have said (1889):

> 'The wave theory of light is, from the point of view of human beings, a certainty.'

a Explain whether you think Hertz would make the same statement today.
b Do you think 'certainty' is ever an appropriate way of labelling a model like the wave model of light? Why?

Q2 'Electrons (and photons) behave in a perfectly definite way. The results to be expected from an experiment can be stated perfectly clearly. The trouble is the results do not seem to be intelligible if one wishes to say that electrons (and photons) behave exactly like something else (a wave, or a particle).'

a What are the results to be expected from, say, a two-slit 'interference' experiment?
b Do these results lead to 'trouble' as suggested above?

Q3 Suppose an electron from an accelerator is observed to travel in a path of radius 50 mm at right angles to a magnetic field B of size 1.0 N A^{-1} m^{-1}. What wavelength is associated with an electron having the momentum implied by these data? Why can the path be seen clearly in a cloud or bubble chamber, unaffected by wave behaviour?

$$h = 6.6 \times 10^{-34} \text{ J s.}$$
$$e = 1.6 \times 10^{-19} \text{ C.}$$
$$Bev = \frac{mv^2}{r}.$$

Q4 A nucleus emits a gamma ray photon, and recoils in the opposite direction from that in which the gamma ray is emitted.

a Why does the nucleus recoil?
b Would a less massive nucleus recoil with more, or less, or the same velocity for the same gamma ray energy?
c Why is the wavelength of the gamma ray a little longer than the wavelength calculated from $E = hf$, and the difference E between the nuclear energy levels concerned in the emission of the gamma ray?

Q5 Give a reason why an electron microscope can be used to form images of objects like viruses, about 10^{-8} m in size, for which an optical microscope is useless.

Q6a Does the velocity of an electron vary with its energy?
  b Does the wavelength associated with an electron vary with its velocity?
  c Does the wavelength associated with an electron vary with its energy?
  d Does the velocity of a photon vary with its energy?
  e Does the wavelength of a photon vary with its energy?
  f Does the wavelength of a photon vary with its velocity?

Q7 A helium ion He^+ and a hydrogen atom both have one electron. The He^+ ion is half the size of the H atom. Suggest a reason why the electron will be harder to remove from the ion than from the atom.

Q8 Why did Rutherford, Geiger, and Marsden not detect diffraction effects when they studied alpha particles fired at a crystal lattice of metal atoms? (Energy of alpha particles used ≈ 1 MeV, $e = 1.6 \times 10^{-19}$ C, mass of alpha particle $\approx 10^{-26}$ kg, $h = 6.6 \times 10^{-34}$ J s.)

Q9 Work on ionic crystals (Unit 3, Part Four), suggests that sodium and chlorine ions are very unsquashable. Why is it hard to squash ions that are, after all, mostly empty space?

Q10 For discussion or comment:

'When people start to learn physics, they usually expect to learn things physicists feel certain to be true. After a while, they find they have learned instead why physicists do not feel absolutely certain of anything.'

Answers

Part One
Photons

1 The wave model. The bright parts of the spectrum are explained by supposing that waves coming from many slits at just the right angle can all add up in phase at this angle, but will cancel at other angles.

2 No. Try a long exposure and see if the exposed/unexposed boundary shifts.

3 Keep film in metal boxes. Gamma rays penetrate paper, and thick lead boxes are needed to protect film from such radiation.

4 Hard to answer briefly. But measurements give scientific thinking something definite to work on. They also tell you when you are wrong, which is very important. It seems likely that a wave-protagonist could explain away our first examples (photography, ionization, photosynthesis) because they are rather vague. But faced with the measured energy of photo-electrons, which does not increase if the light is brighter, he could be in greater difficulties.

5 They are exactly the same: a 'cut off' exists beyond which longer waves have zero effect.

6 $f = 5.8 \times 10^{15}$ Hz, $\lambda = 0.52 \times 10^{-7}$ m (for visible light $\lambda \approx 5 \times 10^{-7}$ m).

7 $\lambda = 5.6 \times 10^{-13}$ m. This is the largest wavelength that will do. Notice that λ is the same order of size as an atomic nucleus.

8 Photon energy $\approx 10^{-23}$ J.
Photons emitted per second $\approx 10^{20}$ s^{-1}.
Photons emitted per cycle $\approx 10^{10}$ ($f = 10^{10}$ Hz).

9 10^7 watts. No: there must be very few of these big photons.

10 No. The evidence came from electron collisions. (You should be able to expand this answer.)

11a To the level at 10.7×10^{-19} J.
  b The violet (short wavelength, high frequency) line must come from the bigger jump.
  c Its photon energy is 6.3×10^{-19} J, close to the ultra-violet photon at 7.84×10^{19} J and bigger than the violet photon of energy 4.56×10^{-19} J. This line will be in the invisible ultra-violet.

12 It would be arguing in a circle (figure 87).

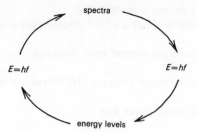

Figure 87

spectra

$E=hf$ $E=hf$

energy levels

13 Maybe, if it goes on being useful, and having the same measured value, in other circumstances. (We shall see that it does.)

14 The (red) line $\lambda = 6.56 \times 10^{-7}$ m appears at the extreme right as a heavy blur (it is very bright). The nearby fine lines are not from H atoms. The line at 3.89×10^{-7} m is nearly in the middle, with at least two more lines visible at shorter wavelengths still. Notice how the lines make a smooth series, getting closer and closer together.

15 The Balmer frequency is the difference between the first two Lyman frequencies. W. Ritz pointed out in 1908 that *all* spectral lines could be expressed as differences in a similar way.

16 A frequency f_3, corresponding to a jump between the two upper levels, where
$$E_2 - E_1 = h(f_2 - f_1)$$
$$f_3 = f_2 - f_1.$$
This is the relationship found in question 15.

17 Lyman (high frequency) lines are like the ABC set, Balmer (lower frequency) lines are like the DE set. Perhaps they all come from the same energy levels except that the Lyman lines all involve a lower level like level 1.

18 Each Balmer frequency is the difference between the Lyman line at 24.659×10^{14} Hz and one other higher line. Each Paschen line is the difference between the Lyman line at 29.226×10^{14} Hz and one higher line.

19 16.3×10^{-19} J.
19.35×10^{-19} J.

20 The difference between the above two energies: 3.05×10^{-19} J.

21 The paper now stretches from level $n = 2$ to the limit. Each level, index number n, lies at $21.8 \times 10^{-19}/n^2$ below the limit.

_____

22 Each photon has energy $\approx 4 \times 10^{-19}$ J.
If the power is 10^{-2} W, that is about 3×10^{16} photons per second.

23 About 10^{12} photons per second enter your eye.

24 About 3×10^{-4} m between photons (10^{-12} second between photons).

25 10^4 times further apart, about 3 m.

Part Two
Electrons

1 The electrons have energy because they are accelerated by a potential difference. At 5 kV and 1 mA, a power of 5 W is delivered. If some electrons are stopped in the thick support material of the target, it will become hot.

2 Red light has a longer wavelength than blue light. Its diffraction pattern is broader.

3 Larger diffraction angles ('broader' patterns) would come from a larger wavelength, given the same spacing of atoms.

4 If the atoms moved apart, the rings would become a little smaller.

5 More slowly.

6 Slow electrons have a larger wavelength than do fast electrons.

7 $d_1 \sin \theta_1 = d_2 \sin \theta_2$ if θ_1 and θ_2 are measured at the same wavelength. The wavelength disappears from the equation, so if d_1/d_2 is constant, $\sin \theta_1 / \sin \theta_2$ is constant. The ring diameters D_1, D_2, are nearly proportional to $\sin \theta_1$, $\sin \theta_2$. So D_1/D_2 measured at any one wavelength should be equal to D_1/D_2 measured at any other wavelength.

8 Smaller ring (smaller $\sin \theta$) from larger spacing ($\lambda = d \sin \theta$). So the smaller ring comes from rows with spacing 1.7 d.

9 $\sqrt{3}$.

10 $\sqrt{3} = 1.73$. The agreement with the sample results is fair.

11 Velocity proportional to $\sqrt{V}$.

12 0.167 radian.

13 0.167 approximately, using the fact that the sine of a small angle is nearly equal to that angle measured in radians.

14 0.205×10^{-10} m.

15 $mv = \sqrt{2mqV}$.

16 3.81×10^{-23} kg m s^{-1}.

17 $h = 7.8 \times 10^{-34}$ J s. (Accepted value 6.6×10^{-34} J s.)

18 Yes. Both are in J s since energy ($\frac{1}{2}mv^2$) can be measured in kg m^2 s^{-2} and momentum (mv) in kg m s^{-1}.

19 It would be some reason.

20 $\lambda \propto 1/\sqrt{V}$. The wavelength is to be raised by a factor of 10^4, so V must be reduced by a factor of 10^8, giving 5×10^{-5} V. It would be impossible to produce and detect electrons with such low energies.

21 $h/\lambda = mv = \sqrt{2mqV}$. Slope is $\lambda V^{\frac{1}{2}} = h/\sqrt{2mq}$.
$h = (\sqrt{2mq}) \times$ slope $= \sqrt{2 \times 9.1 \times 10^{-31} \times 1.6 \times 10^{-19}} \times (12.25 \times 10^{-10}) = 6.61 \times 10^{-34}$ J s.

22 About 2000 times slower, for a neutron is 2000 times more massive than an electron.

23 If mass is of order 0.1 kg, velocity 10 m s^{-1}, $\lambda \approx 10^{-33}$ m.

24 Smaller wavelength – smaller angles; larger wavelength – larger angles. λ for X-rays is about the same as interatomic spacings in crystals. For light the wavelength is much larger, and no diffraction pattern is produced. For tennis balls, a structure of spacing 10^{-33} m would give possible angles but for d (say) 10^{-2} m, $\sin \theta \approx 10^{-31}$.

Part Three
Waves in boxes

1 X-ray diffraction (Unit 1) tells us the spacing between atoms or ions in a solid which, if we assume that each atom is touching some of its neighbours, enables us to work out how big the atoms are.

When gases diffuse through one another, they do so rather slowly because any one molecule keeps hitting others as it travels around. So it takes time for molecules to move from where there are more of them to where there are few of them. From the time needed, compared with the very short time a molecule would take to move unimpeded, the size of the molecules that get in the way can be calculated. This is done in Nuffield O-level Physics, Year IV.

If oil spreads on water, sometimes some oils spread out into a layer one molecule thick. The thickness of the oil carpet can be found if we know its area and the volume of the drop originally placed on water.

2 Standing waves appear: the travelling waves going each way bounce off the fixed ends of the string and interfere with each other.

3 The longest wavelength λ possible is 1 m (half a wavelength on 0.5 m). The lowest frequency f = velocity/λ = 200 Hz.

4 10^{-10} m.

5 Largest. $\lambda \leqslant 4 \times 10^{-10}$ m.

6 mv $\quad 1.6 \times 10^{-24}$ kg m s^{-1}.

7 No. The wavelength given is the largest possible value, the momentum is therefore the least possible value. ($mv \doteq h/\lambda$.)

8 Kinetic energy $\geqslant 14 \times 10^{-19}$ J.

9 The electrical attraction between them.

10 Potential energy = $q_1 q_2/4\pi\varepsilon_0 r$. Energy transferred = 23×10^{-19} J.

11 No. It needs 23×10^{-19} J.

12 Ten times smaller. $\lambda < 0.4 \times 10^{-10}$ m.

13 Ten times larger. $mv > 16 \times 10^{-24}$ kg m s^{-1}.

14 A hundred times larger.

15 1400×10^{-19} J.

16 230×10^{-19} J (ten times as much; potential energy $\propto 1/r$).

17 No. The electron has more kinetic energy than is needed to escape.

18 Energy of order 10^{-12} J.

19 Energy of order 10 MeV (10^7 eV).

20 One only.

21 When you reach a wall your momentum suffers a short, sharp change. If you move without hitting a wall, your momentum is unchanged (you could even be on roller skates, feeling no force at all except at the walls). The only large forces that occur arise when you hit the walls.

22 The electron feels a force towards the proton that varies as $1/r^2$. There is nothing corresponding to a wall which suddenly pushes an outward moving electron back towards the proton. In the whistle-in-a-field situation, you will move as if a force attracts you to the prize. The feebler the sound, the less the 'force' would appear to be, and if the sound dies off as $1/r^2$, the situation might be made into quite a good imitation of electrical attraction.

23 The pit b with shelving sides is more like the $1/r$ variation of potential energy for electrical attraction. The steep sided pit a is like the hard-edged 'box' used in stage one.

24 -46×10^{-19} J (doubled, since r has halved).

25 The closer the electron is to the proton, the smaller its wavelength and so the larger its momentum and kinetic energy. At some small radius r, the rise in kinetic energy is actually bigger than the drop in potential energy, and the electrical attraction fails to pull the electron in as close as this.

26 After 10 metres of vertical rise.

27 At about $r = 1.1 \times 10^{-10}$ m. The kinetic energy is zero.

28 The potential energy falls. The kinetic energy rises.

29 At $r = 0.3 \times 10^{-10}$ m, the potential energy $V = -77 \times 10^{-19}$ J. The kinetic energy is the difference $E - V = 55.2 \times 10^{-19}$ J.

30 Yes.

31 The waves travel most slowly on the thick cord. The tension is the same, so the extra mass per unit length lowers the velocity.

32 $v = f\lambda$, so small v means small λ. The wave doesn't travel far in one cycle.

33a Yes. λ increases as r increases, so this is plausible.
b No. λ is smaller, not larger, at large radius.
c Yes. There is only one loop, but the wave is more sharply curved at small radius.
d No. The wave is more sharply curved at large radius, where the 'wavelength' should be large.

34 Mean $mv \approx 2 \times 10^{-24}$ kg m s^{-1}.

35 Mean $\lambda \approx 3 \times 10^{-10}$ m.

36 The next possible standing wave will have $n = 2$ loops, the next $n = 3$, and so on.

37 $E_2 = \dfrac{E_1}{2^2} = \dfrac{E_1}{4}$.

38 Because $V \propto (1/r)$, and the radius comes where $E = V$. Reducing E and V by a factor 4 raises r by a factor 4.

39 Mean wavelength $= 2 \times$ (radius)/(number of loops). For $n = 1$, $\lambda_1 = 2r/1$ and for $n = 2$, $\lambda_2 = 2 \times 4r/2 = 4r$.

40 The mean momentum is halved.

41 The mean wavelength has doubled, as it must if the wave is to fit.

42 ZYX.

43 b.

44 b.

45 b.

Answers to 'More questions'

1a We don't think he would be so sure, though the case must have seemed cut and dried at the time. The whole of Part One, 'Photons', was about why the wave model on its own is not good enough.

  b How could one ever know that all the predictions of a particular model had been tested? The history of physics has been full of surprises for those who felt 'sure'.

2a Electrons (photons) arrive one by one, in random places, building up so that the number arriving at a place averages out to be proportional to the intensity of a wave to be expected to arrive at that place.

  b It depends what you call 'trouble'. If you insist on one of the two models alone, wave or particle, the predictions are wrong. If you mix the two 'correctly', the predictions are right, but you may not like the mixture.

3 $\lambda = 0.8 \times 10^{-13}$ m. The wavelength is too small to see diffraction effects on this scale.

4a The gamma ray carries off momentum; to conserve momentum the nucleus must recoil, as must a gun firing a shell.

  b More.

c The nucleus carries off some of the energy E; the gamma ray must have less than E and so have longer wavelength from $E = hf$ (or you could argue from the Doppler effect).

5 Electron wavelengths $\lambda = h/mv$ are much smaller than 10^{-8} m for realistic energies. The wavelength of visible light is larger than 10^{-8} m.

6a Yes.
  b Yes.
  c Yes.
  d No.
  e Yes.
  f Not in empty space. In glass, though, which disperses light having a range of wavelengths, the speed and wavelength are related.

7 The electron is both closer to the nucleus, and the nucleus has twice the pulling power (charge $2e$).

8 The wavelength is too small. ($\lambda \approx 10^{-14}$ m.)

9 To squash an atom or ion means confining its electrons within a smaller space. This raises the kinetic energy, for λ must decrease and mv increase. This energy has to be supplied by the squashing forces.

10 We don't know how you feel. But this is how it seems to some of us. If it is true, it is a good thought with which to end a physics course.

Lists of films, film loops, books, and apparatus

Films and film loops
16 mm films

The following three black and white, sound films are available for hire from Guild Sound and Vision Ltd (formerly Sound Services Ltd.), Kingston Road, Merton Park, London S.W.19. The last two are the most useful of the three. All originate from the PSSC programme.

'Photons.' 19 minutes, black and white, sound. No. 900 4173–2.
'Interference of photons.' 14 minutes, black and white, sound. No. 900 4174–9.
'Matter waves.' 28 minutes, black and white, sound. No. 900 4177–0.

8 mm film loops

The following computer-made loop is essential for those who wish to attempt Part Three, stage three, of this Unit. 'Solving a standing wave equation for a hydrogen atom.' Longman (standard 8).

The following two loops may be useful, but are not essential.
'Vibrations of a drum.' Ealing Scientific, No. A80-3924/1 (super 8).
'Soap film oscillations.' Ealing Scientific, No. A80-2660/1 (super 8).

Books

Page numbers of references in this book appear in bold type.

For teachers

In writing this Unit we have drawn with gratitude on the ideas of three major contributions to the teaching of quantum ideas. Each of them is worth studying. They are:

Mott, N. F. (1968) 'On teaching quantum phenomena', from *Sources of physics teaching*, Part 1. Taylor & Francis. **88**.
This contains reprints from the journal *Contemporary physics*.

PSSC (1966) *Advanced topics supplement.* Heath,
now incorporated into
PSSC (1968) *College physics.* Raytheon. **21, 57, 74, 118, 125**.

Sherwin, C. W. (1961) *Basic concepts of physics.* Holt, Rinehart & Winston. **64**.
This is out of print at the time of writing, but it contains so much of value that we list it in the hope that it will be reprinted.

Teachers will also find much of value in:

Boorse, H. A., and Motz, L. (1966) *The world of the atom*, Volume 1. Basic Books. **54, 64**.
This is an interesting collection of papers from the Greeks to the present day, but is an expensive investment.

Feynman, R. P., Leighton, R. B., Sands, M. (1963) *The Feynman lectures on physics,* Volume 1. Addison-Wesley. **3, 40, 57, 71**.

Cropper, W. H. (1970) *The quantum physicists.* Oxford University Press.

Wichmann, E. H. (1971) Berkeley Physics Course, Volume 4 *Quantum physics.* McGraw-Hill.

For students

In addition to parts of Feynman *et al, The Feynman lectures on physics* (see above) and PSSC *College physics* (see above), the following are useful:

Bennet, G. A. G. (1968) *Electricity and modern physics.* MKS edition. Edward Arnold. **58**.

Born, M. (1951) *The restless Universe.* Dover. **42, 57, 64, 138**.

Caro, D. E., McDonell, J. A., and Spicer, B. M. (1962) *Modern physics.* Edward Arnold. **58, 64**.

Classical scientific papers – physics (1964) Mills & Boon. **118**.

Conn, G. K. T., and Turner, H. D. (1965) *The evolution of the nuclear atom.* Iliffe. **64**.

Hoffmann, B. (1970) *The strange story of the quantum.* Penguin. Also available in Dover Press edition. **58**.

Millikan, R. A. (1963) Phoenix Science Series *The electron.* University of Chicago Press. **11**.

Open University (1971) Science Foundation Course, Units 6 and 7, *Atoms, elements, and isotopes: atomic structure. The electronic structure of atoms.* Open University Press.

Project Physics (1970) Text and Reader, Unit 5, *Models of the atom.* Holt, Rinehart & Winston, N.Y. **39, 58, 138**.

PSSC (1965) *Physics.* 2nd edition. Heath. **21, 39, 42, 57**.

Rogers, E. M. (1960) *Physics for the inquiring mind.* Oxford University Press. **15, 42, 57, 64, 138**.

Rothman, M. A. (1966) *The laws of physics.* Penguin. **58**.

Tolansky, S. (1968) *Revolution in optics.* Penguin. **58**.

Toulmin, S., and Goodfield, J. (1965) *The architecture of matter.* Penguin. **58**.

Apparatus list

		Experiment
14	e.h.t power supply	10.5, 10.7
27	transformer	10.7
44/2	G-clamp (small)	10.8
50/1	cylindrical magnet	10.7
52 A	flashlamp bulb 1.25 V, 0.25 A	10.6
52 B	U2 cell	10.6
52 C	baseboard	10.6
52 D	spring connector with lampholder	10.6
52 K	crocodile clip	10.1
59	l.t. variable voltage supply	10.2
69	high dispersion prism	10.2
121	metal strips as jaws	10.8
130/1	scaler	10.3, 10.10
130/3	GM tube holder	10.3, 10.10
130/6	gamma GM tube	10.3, 10.10
134/2	xenon flasher	10.8, 10.9
189	ultra-violet lamp	10.1
191/1	coarse grating	10.6
191/2	fine grating	10.4, 10.5
193/2	hydrogen spectrum tube	10.5
194	holder for spectrum tubes	10.5
195/1	pure gamma source	10.3, 10.10
197	electron diffraction tube	10.7
503–6	retort stand base, rod, boss, and clamp	10.1, 10.4, 10.8
512/2	beaker 400 cm³	10.10
1000	leads	10.1, 10.2, 10.5, 10.8
1003/1	milliammeter (1 mA)	10.1, 10.2
1006	electrometer	10.1, 10.2
1009	signal generator	10.8, 10.9
1033	cell holder with four U2 cells	10.1
1033	cell holder with one U2 cell	10.2
1044	large loudspeaker	10.8
1053	*Local purchase items*	
	razor blade	10.1
	card with slit	10.2
	strip of fluorescent paper, 20 mm wide, 0.5 m long, green	10.4
	fogged photographic film	10.6
	cardboard slide mounts 35 mm	10.6
	sheet of rubber	10.8
1055	*Small laboratory items*	
	glass plate	10.1
	wire gauze, 70 mm × 60 mm, for example, 20 mesh copper	10.1

	microscope slide	10.4
	photographic exposure meter	10.6
	length of light chain	10.9
	V-shaped strip of rubber	10.9
	rubber cord (0.5 m long, 3 mm square cross section)	10.8, 10.9
	light rubber cord (0.5 m long, e.g. dressmaking elastic)	10.9
1056	*Chemicals*	
	magnesium ribbon, 100 mm long	10.1
	a little mercury in a polythene bottle	10.4
1060	vibrator	10.8, 10.9
1067 E	set of stops	10.2
1068	parallel beam projector	10.2
1069	apparatus for showing the Compton effect	10.10
1071	mercury discharge lamp	10.4
1073	concave reflecting grating	10.4
1074	photo-electric cell	10.2
1076	large ring	10.8

Index

Where significant information is contained in an illustration or diagram, the page reference is italicized.

A

alpha decay, 129–31
apparatus, 162–3
atomic nucleus, 72–5
atomic number, 118
atoms, size of, 63, 68, 70–71
  stability of, 62–3

B

Balmer, Johann, 28
Bohr, Niels, quoted, 29
Bohr theory, 64, 93
bond angles, 127–8
books and further reading, 3, 11, 21, 54,
  57–9, 64, 74, 118, 138
Born, Max, 94, 134
Bragg, Sir William, quoted, 39
Broglie, L. de, 51, 52, 94

C

chance, 34–5, 131
  see also Units 5, 9
compressibility, 72, 147
Compton effect, 16, 138–43
computer-generated film, 107–11
covalent bonding, 127

D

deuterons, 16, 73, 74
diffraction, 6, 30, 31–3, 56
  see also electrons; X-ray; and Units 1 and 8
Dirac, P.A.M., 94, 98
  quoted, 113

E

Einstein, A., quoted, 5, 10–11, 39
electrons, 41–60, 72, 76–81
  diffraction of, 42, 44, 45–51, 53
  wavelength and momentum of, 51–2, 54, 55
energy levels, 21
  of deuteron, 73
  of hydrogen, 24–9, 90–92
  of mercury, 19, 20, 21
  of nuclei, 75
  see also Unit 2
exclusion principle, 120

F

Feynman, R.P., quoted, 3, 40
film loops, 68
films, 29, 56, 107–11

G

gamma rays, 7, 15, 16, 73
  see also Compton effect
graphite, 128
  electron diffraction by, 47–51, 53

H

Heisenberg, W., 94, 134
helium, 11, 118–20
  He^+ ion, 114–17, 147
Hertz, G., 10
Hooke, R., quoted, 41
hydrogen, 147
  Bohr theory of, 64, 93
  H_2^+ molecule, 125–7
  size of atom of, 63, 70–71
  spectrum of, 22–9; $1/n^2$ rule, 90–92
  wave theory of, 69–71, 74, 76–9, 86–90;
    film illustrating, 107–11; Schrödinger
    equation for, 101, 102–6; wave states
    for, 120, 121

I

iodine molecule, 121
ionic crystals, 68, 147
  see also Unit 3
ionization, 7, 11
ionization energy, 26, 120

L

light, dual model of, 6, 33, 38–40
  see also diffraction; photons
lithium, 118–20

M

matrix mechanics, 134
mercury, spectrum of, 17–21; see also
  Units 2, 5
microwaves, 15, 16
Millikan, R.A., 11
molecules, bonding in, 125–7
  oscillating, 121–5
Morrison, P., quoted, 61
Moseley, H.G.J., 118

N

neutrons, 55, 72, 73
Newton, Isaac, quoted, 5

O

optical grids, 49
orbitals, 93
oscillators, variable-wavelength, 81–4

P

Pauli exclusion principle, 120
Periodic Table, 120
photo-electric effect, 6, 8–11, 33
    colour and intensity effects in, 11–15
    time effects in, 37
    see also Unit 5
photographic quality, *36*, 37
photons, 5–39
    counting of, 16
    emission of, 17–21
    energies of, 15
    momentum of, 52
    random behaviour of, 34–5, 37
    see also Compton effect
photosynthesis, 8
Planck constant (h), 13, 15, 21, 52, 53, 54
polythene, diffraction by, *42*
potential well, 77–8, 79
protons, 72, 73, 78–9

Q

quantitative experiments, 8
quantum theory, 22, 92–4, 134–5
    see also Schrödinger equation

R

radio waves, 15
radioactivity, 129–31
    see also Unit 5
randomness, *see* chance
reading, uses of, 4, 56–7
    see also books and further reading
repulsion forces, 72
    see also Unit 3
rubber, *42*

S

Schrödinger, Erwin, 93, 94
Schrödinger equation, 79, 95–102, 134–5
    difficulties of solution, 112
    solution for hydrogen, 102–6; film
        illustrating, 107–11
sodium chloride, 68
    see also Unit 3
solids, incompressibility of, 72, 147
spectra, 6–7
    of hydrogen, 22–9
    of ionized helium, 114–17
    of mercury, 17–21
    see also Units 2, 5
standing waves, 65–8
    spherically symmetrical, 84–5
    variable-wavelength, 81–4

T

Taylor, G. I., 33
Thomson, G. P., 51
tunnel diode, 131

W

water molecule, 127–8
wave mechanics, *see* quantum theory

X

X-ray spectra, 117–18
X-rays, 7
    diffraction of, *42*, *43*
    wavelength of, 33

Y

Young, T., quoted, 5